50

YALE
ADMISSION
SUCCESS
STORIES

Also by the Staff of the *Yale Daily News*

The Insider's Guide to the Colleges

50

YALE

ADMISSION

SUCCESS

STORIES

And the Essays That Made
Them Happen

The Staff of the
Yale Daily News

ST. MARTIN'S GRIFFIN
New York

First published in the United States by St. Martin's Griffin, an imprint of St. Martin's Publishing Group

www.stmartins.com

Library of Congress Cataloging-in-Publication Data

Title: 50 Yale admission success stories : and the essays that made them happen / The Staff of the *Yale Daily News*.
Other titles: Fifty Yale admission success stories | Yale daily news.
Description: First Edition. | New York : St. Martin's Griffin, 2020. |
Identifiers: LCCN 2019037606 | ISBN 9781250248794 (trade paperback) | ISBN 9781250248800 (ebook)
Subjects: LCSH: College applications—United States. | Essays. | Yale University.
Classification: LCC LB2351.52.U6 A14 2020 | DDC 378.1/616—dc23
LC record available at https://lccn.loc.gov/2019037606

Our books may be purchased in bulk for promotional, educational, or business use. Please contact your local bookseller or the Macmillan Corporate and Premium Sales Department at 1-800-221-7945, extension 5442, or by email at MacmillanSpecialMarkets@macmillan.com.

First Edition: March 2020

10 9 8 7 6 5 4 3 2 1

Acknowledgments & Credits

50 Yale Success Stories Executive Director: Yeama Ho
Publisher: Eric Foster
Editor-in-Chief: Britton O'Daly

Lead Illustrator: Sonia Ruiz
Lead Editors: Joshua Gonzalez, Lucy Silbaugh

Profile Authors: Nathalie Bussemaker, Isabel Bysiewicz, Sophia Catsambi, Aakshi Chaba, Serena Cho, Lindsay Daugherty, Adelaide Feibel, Hailey Fuchs, Raymond Gao, Chloé Glass, Ashna Gupta, Eui Young Kim, Julianna Lai, Kyung Mi Lee, Madison Mahoney, Jever Mariwala, Skakel McCooey, Jane Miller, Caroline Moore, Zoe Nuechterlein, Britton O'Daly, Alice Park, Anastasiia Posnova, Asha Prihar, Keshav Raghavan, Meera Rothman, Carolyn Sacco, Razan Sulieman, Rianna Turner, Will Wang, Carly Wanna, Sammy Westfall, Angela Xiao, Amy Xiong

Illustrations Editors: Keyi Cui, Valerie Navarrete
Staff Illustrators: Marc Boudreaux, Lauren Gatta, Michelle M. Li, Zihao Lin, Claire Mutchnik, Vera Villanueva
Contributing Illustrators: Veronica Chen, Isabel Lee, Valerie Pavilonis

Copy Editors: Maddie Bender, Selena Lee, Alan Liu, Keshav Raghavan

Business Team: Josh Brooks, Nathan Chang, Hunter Contos, James Grad, Hope Newberry, Leah Xiao, Amanda Zhang

Copy Staffers: Mary Chen, Queenie Huang, Isabella Li, Jeffrey Ma, Kinga Obartuch, Shannon Sommers

Contributing Editors: Hana Davis, Caleb Rhodes

Publisher Emeritus: Elizabeth Liu
Editor-in-Chief Emeritus: Rachel Treisman

Special Thanks: Peter Dwoskin, Emad Haerizadeh, Melinda Beck, John Zucker, and the Yale Daily News Foundation

Introduction

If there's one lesson we hope this book teaches you, it is that Yale—like most top-tier liberal arts colleges—does not want its applicants to be one person. This exposition of fifty Yale students is not intended to tell you to try to become just like them. On the contrary, we are here to show you how breathtakingly different from one another Yale students are and that there is no particular attribute or background anyone has to have to be admitted here—other than intellectual passion and excitement about engaging with the world. There is, in other words, no one "Yale type" whom admissions officers seek among the tens of thousands of college applications that flood in each year. There is no moment when an admissions officer throws your Yale application into the garbage because your parents didn't go to college, or because you didn't have enough community service on your application, or because nobody from your high school has ever gone to a school like Yale before. If they did, then a class of roughly sixteen-hundred identical first-year students would stream into the Gothic courtyards of Yale every year.

The wide-ranging undergraduate curriculum that exposes Yale students to all manner of academic experiences each year would be criminally underutilized if incoming classes were so homogenous. Our fourteen residential colleges would be indistinguishable in their traditions, architecture, and subtle quirks. And forget about the thousands of goofy homemade graduation caps that we see at Commencement each May. Where there is no diversity of interests or backgrounds, there is definitely no Yale. (And we at the *Yale Daily News*, for absence of anything interesting to write about, would definitely be out of a job.)

But, thankfully, Yale is a vibrant, dynamic, and powerfully diverse place. Yale's fourteen residential colleges, analogous to student dorms, each offers its own special microcosm of the wider undergraduate community. You do not apply for a spot in a residential college. Instead, incoming students are sorted into colleges at random such that each college, such as Branford or Silliman, represents the full diversity of the Yale undergraduate community as a whole. There is no "athlete" college, or "nerd" or "party" or "science" college, because every college has all of these students, living side by side in intimate suites. Each college has its own wild band of students, held together by sheer love of their newfound, completely arbitrary home, filled with other classmates who adhere to no uniform creed or life path.

We also take our liberal arts identity very seriously. You do not, as you will surely hear, come to Yale to just study computer science or theater. You come here to develop your own intellectual curiosity and let that take the wheel. Most Yale students take approximately thirty-six courses over their four years. With hardly a tenth of students pursuing a double major, and no minors available at Yale, a typical Yale student spends about one third of their time completing their major requirements—and then spends the remaining two thirds taking classes from all over the university. With the rise of interdisciplinary majors at Yale, like Computing & the Arts; Ethics, Politics, & Economics; and Mathematics & Philosophy, even a student's major courses might be spread across many departments. Some students may also elect to take more than four years to complete their undergraduate degree. The university is relatively flexible with students taking a semester or two off, whether it be for gap year traveling, for working, or for health or personal reasons.

We haven't even mentioned all the extracurricular interests that come alive at night—and even sometimes during the day—

at Yale. Dwight Hall, America's oldest collegiate public service institution, supports student organizations that lead community service efforts across southern Connecticut. Mechanical engineers, designers, and "makers" collaborate twenty-four hours a day in the Center for Engineering Innovation & Design (CEID), a staffed and well-resourced makerspace for students to pursue personal, extracurricular, or academic projects using sophisticated machinery. Yale is the only place in the world, students joke, where 2D printing costs ten cents per page, but 3D printing is free. Singers, debaters, aspiring doctors, software engineers—all of them find their niche here through the hundreds of active student groups at Yale.

You will find students in this book who hail from radically different worlds, spanning everywhere from the public schools of New Haven to America's rural heartland to Singapore. You will learn about what brought them to apply to Yale and, hopefully, that revelation will help inform your own decision to apply to Yale or any other college on your radar. You will read the college essays written by these students and, very quickly, witness not only how a compelling college application looks, but also how the thrust of any successful essay in the college admissions process hinges on some level of emotional vulnerability: Schools, Yale as well as others, want to see you as not only eloquent but as honest and mature as well.

Do not try to be the perfect applicant. No admissions committee, anywhere, believes that any high school student is perfect. It is far easier, and far more convincing, to just show yourself to be someone who will uniquely contribute to Yale's community and to convey that you see something special about Yale that will help you to advance in life toward your larger goals. A response to "Why does Yale appeal to you?" should include more than just a perfunctory mention of Yale's residential college system or its liberal arts curriculum; it should show why a Yale education matters to *you*.

Challenge yourself to reach a moment of genuine realization

about your life. Let the profiles and essays in this book inspire you, but do not let them cage in your own approach to Yale. Once again, Yale did not accept these people because they checked off specific boxes for what the ideal Yale candidate looks like. They were accepted because these applicants showed how much they want to experience while at Yale, what they want to give to Yale, and why they need to go to Yale to truly realize their potential.

Developing a strong college application is not about making your best effort to copy the essays of successful applicants who have come before you. It is, however, about taking a chance on your own self, and we genuinely believe that reading this book will help all college applicants, not just those who apply to Yale, realize what they need to draw out of themselves to put together the college application that best communicates the value of who they are. As we said in the beginning, anyone—and we mean *anyone*—can apply to Yale. That means you, too. We wish you the best of luck.

—*The Staff of the* Yale Daily News

A Note on
College Application Essays

Like most U.S. colleges and universities, Yale accepts the Common App ("Common App") for undergraduate admission. The Common App provides a single web portal that allows high school students to apply to multiple colleges without needing to reenter their information each time. Importantly, the Common App also includes an essay component, which almost every college using the application portal requires applicants to submit. The Common App essay currently has seven prompts that are typically repeated each year and are reviewed and updated every few years. Applicants choose one of the seven prompts and write a 650-word personal statement responsive to the prompt. Unlike most other college application essays, the Common App essay is *not* intended to show the applicant's interest in a particular institution. Instead, it provides a broad overview of who the applicant is and showcases the applicant's writing style. This book includes many Common App essays to give you a broader sense of who Yale students are and how they view and describe their identity outside a Yale-specific context.

In addition to the Common App essays, Yale also requires applicants to submit additional essays specific to Yale—these are often referred to as supplements. Since these essays are sent only to Yale, the responses should show the applicant's interest in Yale in particular. Yale's supplement essay prompts have changed slightly over the past few years, but generally fluctuate around the same general themes and tackle the same topics. This book exhibits applicants spanning across four years and their responses to a variety of essay prompts, thus exposing you to a greater variety of ideas and writing.

Throughout the book, we refer to the students by the class year they were in when we first began compiling this book. Accordingly, the first-years are in the class of 2021 and applied in the 2016–2017 application cycle, the sophomores are in the class of 2020 and applied in the 2015–2016 application cycle, and so on. We have organized this book into sections based on the students' class years, and listed the prompts for that specific application cycle at the beginning of each section. Though the essays do vary between years, reading the supplements presented in this book would still undoubtedly be a great resource for planning your own essays.

Some institutions, including Yale, require applicants to write an additional essay if they indicate interest in a STEM (science, technology, engineering, and mathematics) major. Only some applicants need to write this additional essay, but we have included some here for aspiring STEM students to understand what Yale considers to be compelling in this unique essay.

Finally, please keep in mind that we have made as few edits as possible to the essays featured in this book because we want to provide examples of actual college application essays that helped students get into Yale. Although there may be some grammatical errors, we prioritized upholding the integrity of the original essays, as they reflect the constraints and restrictions that limit all applicants, such as word count, paragraph form, and text-stylization options. The essays you will see in this book most accurately represent how the essays arrived on the desks of the admissions officers. All in all, our purpose for compiling this book is to demystify the college application process and make it more transparent for prospective students.

First-Years

Pascale Bradley

Hometown: New York City, NY

Year: First-Year

College: Berkeley

Major(s): English; French

Extracurriculars: Yale Political Union; Yale Francophone Association

PROFILE

Pascale Bradley had Yale on her radar long before she was old enough to apply. Her mom graduated from Yale in 1988, and Pascale knew that she was interested in attending a school with a high academic profile. She applied to eleven schools during the college application process, including Harvard, Brown, Columbia, and Georgetown, in addition to Yale.

When considering colleges, Pascale looked for schools that could meet both her academic and social expectations. She hoped to find a school with a robust anthropology program, but also a campus that had a diverse student body and a spirit of inclusivity.

"I got the sense that at most other schools, social life was more divisive," she says. "At Yale, there was a strong sense of an on-campus community."

Ultimately deciding that Yale checked all of her boxes, she applied for early admission. She was initially deferred, but received and accepted an offer from Yale in the spring.

During her high school career, Pascale was a dedicated three-season runner (cross country in the fall, indoor track in the winter, and outdoor track in the spring). She volunteered with several community service groups, one of which eventually inspired her Common App essay and planted the initial seed for her interest in anthropology.

Eager to continue her community service work at Yale, Pascale immediately joined a service group, First-Years in Service. Although she found the work to be starkly different from the kind she had participated in throughout high school, Pascale had a positive experience with the group. "I expected to be doing more work that involved interacting with people, but I've spent more time learning the administrative side of service work," she explains. Although she initially thought that she would join a running club at Yale, she later realized that she wasn't interested in the daily commitment of running in addition to her other activities and classes. Another surprise emerged in the form of her major: While Pascale entered Yale thinking she would most likely study either anthropology or Ethnicity, Race, & Migration, she got hooked on English after taking a class on Shakespeare's comedies and romances and is now double majoring in English and French.

The social life at Yale, however, was what proved to be Pascale's favorite part of the experience. She raves about her residential college and loves the friends and connections she's made there. Her favorite memories of her first year are from the small courtyard outside her dorm, where fellow first-years would congregate to chat between and after classes.

"I've made so many friends through Berkeley that I might not have met otherwise," Pascale affirms. "The social life at Yale has exceeded my expectations."

Pascale's essays include her Common App personal statement.

ESSAY 1 (COMMON APP):
PERSONAL STATEMENT

I'm standing on a New York City playground on a particularly bright Monday morning in mid-July. The grin on Farrah's face reminds me that it's her birthday. Decked out from head to toe in *Frozen*-themed clothing, she runs over to me to show me her birthday presents. She opens her backpack and pulls out three *Frozen* dolls, still inside their packaging. Later, as the class is about to head to the pool, it dawns on Sebastian that he does not have his towel. I dig through a heap of clothing, swimsuits, and goggles until I find a white towel embroidered with Sebastian's name in blue thread. It looks just like the towel several of my friends own. At lunch that day, Khodi, a precocious five-year-old, invites me to sit with her. I stare into her lunchbox. A note from her mother is squeezed between a star-shaped sandwich and a reusable container of strawberries. The red ink reads, "Have a great day, Khodi! Love, Mommy."

Just a month later, I'm sitting in a tiny kitchen across the country. Jamin inhales three helpings of chicken with steamed vegetables even though he's only two years old and should not have such a large appetite. The teachers exchange worried glances, and I suspect that he did not eat breakfast that morning or dinner the night before. Suzette spills sauce on her sweater, and I grab a napkin to blot the stain. The sauce does not look out of place on her shirt, which she has worn for the past three days. In the afternoon, I play with a two-year-old named Yari. No matter how many books I read to her or how many words I ask her to repeat, she still hasn't learned to speak.

In July, I volunteered at Summer Steps, a program that prepares low-income, mostly minority, New York City preschoolers for kindergarten. The children receive scholarships for kindergarten at independent schools. The teachers, the other volunteers, and I helped the children with their reading and writing skills. In August, I volunteered at Storyteller Children's Center in Santa Barbara, California. The center provides daycare and enrichment to homeless families making less than $10,000 a year. For three weeks, I played with the toddlers so their parents could work or look for work. It occurred to me that while the families at both Summer Steps and Storyteller were considered low-income, the children were living extraordinarily different lives.

When Farrah, Sebastian, and Khodi were juxtaposed with Jamin, Suzette, and Yari, I realized that poverty was more intricate than I had imagined. These faces taught me about the nuances of the term "low-income." There has always been an anthropologist in me, and the children at Summer Steps and Storyteller made me want to use my passion for anthropology as a means of advocacy. When I observed Jamin's appetite, I realized how much work there is left to do.

Ko Lyn Cheang

Hometown: Singapore

Year: First-Year

College: Grace Hopper

Major(s): Philosophy

Extracurriculars: Yale Debate Association;
Yale Daily News staff writer

PROFILE

Ko Lyn Cheang hails from Singapore, but she knew early on that there was more to her future than settling down in her home country. In Singapore, Ko Lyn explains, college education is largely defined by majors, and career opportunities lean heavily toward law and medicine. "Going to a Singaporean university would have been the practical thing to do," she acknowledges. "But I wanted to chase after my dreams."

Ko Lyn, who is a philosophy major, says she sees college not as a preprofessional training ground but as a place where she can ask bigger questions about humanity. Her interest in philosophy truly bloomed only after she arrived at Yale, and Ko Lyn hasn't looked back since, having already declared her major as a rising sophomore.

On weekends, Ko Lyn sometimes travels to other states for debate tournaments with her fellow Yale Debate Association members. During the week, however, she is content to curl up in the library with her readings. Indeed, she wholeheartedly admits that many of her favorite spots on campus are in libraries; she rhapsodizes about the Slavic Reading Room and the circulation-desk hold shelves in Sterling Memorial Library.

"The moment you enter Sterling, the light comes washing down on you through the mosaic, almost like an intimate, spiritual experience," Ko Lyn says. "It makes you think that the essays you write here are part of a greater project in the pursuit of knowledge."

Ko Lyn also writes for the *Yale Daily News*, an experience that allows her to venture outside the restraints of typical student life. She describes journalism as providing her with a window into others' lives; for instance, one of Ko Lyn's favorite stories allowed her to interview a former Japanese geisha who is now a language instructor at Yale.

Indeed, since she arrived at Yale, Ko Lyn has been especially impressed and surprised by the general campus attitude toward sharing stories—both people's receptiveness to others' stories and their willingness to share their own. She has found her peers at Yale to be curious and open-minded listeners, quick to appreciate the many facets that comprise a person's life.

Ko Lyn says this tendency toward empathy stands in stark contrast to her experience in Singapore, where, she reflects, people are understood less by the experiences that have shaped them than by their social status or economic power. She believes that cursory, one-dimensional measures like these are appealing because they are simple—but they are also less revealing.

Ko Lyn sees how this disparity comes to bear on the college process, too. She wishes that she could tell her high school self to focus on the storytelling aspect of the college application, especially where the essay is concerned. She urges students to use this space as an opportunity for some "deep soul-searching" and real self-reflection. "You have to distill yourself into a 500-word piece that captures the essence of who you are," she says. "It's daunting but rewarding in the end."

Ko Lyn's essays include her Common App personal statement and two of her Yale supplemental essays.

ESSAY 1 (COMMON APP):
PERSONAL STATEMENT

Sarong kebaya embroidered with the passionate patois of Peranakan people. Qipao silken as lilting Mandarin. Language is the clothes on your back, the shoes on your feet, but I often feel undressed. My Chinese parents speak Malay as their mother tongue, the vernacular language in this part of Southeast Asia. Singapore, trading post of Asia, pedals language. Here, English is more valuable than saffron, more coveted than oil. I am proof of its currency, Straits-Chinese girl, who feels more at home reciting Shakespeare's sonnets than those of Li Bai, who can apprehend Hume and Eliot's philosophy but struggles to wring meaning from *san zi jing,* the aphoristic three-word classics that every child in China memorizes by age six.

At four, my parents enlist the help of a Chinese tutor from Urumqi. She wears a silk shawl and knits Chinese idioms into her lilting speech. Singapore's bilingual policy mandates that every child learn his or her "mother tongue," or ethnic language, as a way to stay rooted. During those weekly Mandarin lessons, I never felt rooted. Oh Singapore, is this how you feel? Island of 3 million, who needs something to moor her ashore, lest she drift into the South China Sea. The longer I trained my gaze on the Mandarin characters before me, the more they swam like dark tadpoles, eluding my capture.

As a kid, I joked: my mother does not even speak my mother tongue, so how *can* it be my mother tongue? The joke stops being funny when I fail my first Chinese *ting xie,* dictation exam, and walk home with tears sizzling like hot oil. As I grow older and learn about the ethnic conflict in Urumqi's melting pot of Muslim and Han Chinese cultures, I wonder if my Chinese teacher can teach me how to bridge worlds too. Singapore is an island of flotsam, of immigrants like my grandmother jettisoned blindly from their native lands. Even as I master the English language, it feels like a borrowed book in my hand, due for return to someone else's library. I let English words roll off my tongue like tropical rain falling from a British sky. Heart hammering, I anticipate when people will call me out—*fraud! thief!*—and drag me incontinent into the Chinese Room.

At fifteen, I decide to learn Russian. This language, of Northern winters and dramatic personalities, mesmerized me. Russian ignited my imagination in a way my fifteen years of Mandarin never did. Russian's hard edge chipped against Mandarin's soft toffee. Where Mandarin feathered like the edge of sleep, Russian bellowed military commands, jolting me wide awake. I plunged into learning, liberated of Mandarin's ancestral baggage. I owed this new language my heartfelt dedication to learning. The linguistic distinctions were odd but fascinating. Russian gives nouns genders; every word is a person—unique, mutable, inflected to carry new import. In Chinese, words are pebbles of self-contained meaning. Fathoming Mandarin words into sentences was like playing a game of tangram, rearranging characters to form the desired shape. Russian is more like a tango; words fleet-footed, the dance ephemeral. I found a kindred spirit in Russian. Like me, it is evolving. Mandarin now felt like a pair of old beaded slippers.

In Mandarin, we have an idiom for leaving home: lixiang-beijing. When translated literally, it means 'to leave home with your back facing the well'. To go away from home is to scale the well in which I was born. A frog at the bottom of the well is blissful in its inexperience. I am not one language, not confined to one narrow sect of humanity. My back is to the well; I shed my old beaded slippers and don a traveller's coat of many colours. The yellow brick road vanishes in my wake. In its place, stretching for miles, is a technicolour sky.

ESSAY 2 (YALE SUPPLEMENT): WHY DO THESE AREAS APPEAL TO YOU?
(LITERATURE, ANTHROPOLOGY)

Literature and anthropology are telescopes into the past; philosophy, a prism into the mind. I want to ask the hard questions: Do I have free will? Is meaning lost in translation? Is there eternal truth? What is an "I"? Am I my mind, body or something more? Literature is an empathetic account of the past, anthropology a scientific documentation of human lives. I want to find commonality in lives separated by time and space, find meaning within them, partake in the collective memory of humanity, and interrogate what it means to be human.

ESSAY 3 (YALE SUPPLEMENT): WHY DOES YALE APPEAL TO YOU?

Passionate about finding solutions to tackle climate change, I admire how Yale, a member of the Global Carbon Pricing Leadership Coalition, spearheads the sustainability movement. In reading about Yale's discourse on race, discrimination and free speech, I admire and yearn to contribute to the Yale spirit of interrogating the status quo. I am invigorated by the recent Yale Dramat play *The Architecture of Rain*, unprecedented for its all Asian-American cast. I, too, aspire to bring my Singaporean perspective to Yale's ongoing conversation—in the art I make, plays I write and in sides of a debate I represent.

Allison Chen

Hometown: Chandler, AZ

Year: First-Year

College: Morse

Major(s): Economics; History

Extracurriculars: Yale Building Bridges,
co-president;
The Yale Politic, editor;
The Yale Globalist, editor

PROFILE

Allison Chen believes that who she is today is a consequence of two main factors: Her Chinese upbringing and her love for Spanish culture, which she developed in middle school. Through Chinese dancing lessons and Spanish literature classes—plus her involvement in Model UN and student government in high school—Allison discovered a real passion for global affairs.

Now at Yale, Allison—who grew up in Chandler, Arizona—is double majoring in economics and history, with a specialization in international and diplomatic history. She also keeps her interests alive through the arts, especially theater and writing. A member of the Yale Dramatic Association, she has participated in numerous productions, and she regularly writes for three campus publications: the *Yale Daily News*, the *Yale Globalist*, and the *Yale Politic*.

Allison also tries to spend some time doing things that do

not involve school or her extracurriculars. She says she loves walking down Broadway and exploring its many shops—the Yale Bookstore is her favorite place to browse. The year-end Spring Fling music festival held on Old Campus stands out as one of Allison's favorite moments from her first year at Yale. She loved how the event gave people the chance to spend time with one another for a day without worrying about upcoming paper deadlines and exams.

In thinking about how her productive, academic self and her personal, fun-loving self coalesce, Allison still thinks of Spanish painter Francisco Goya's *Saturn Devouring His Son*, which captured her attention as a young student (and about which she wrote one of her Yale supplemental essays). She loves the dual registers on which the painting operates. It marks an important transition in the art world while also telling a compelling story. And Allison's own history with the painting contains these two elements, too—the raw and unjustified curiosity she felt toward it as a child, as well as the intellectual and informed way she was able to engage with it as an adult. Allison feels that it perfectly expressed who she was as a child, and who she still is today.

Allison's essays include one of her Yale supplemental essays.

ESSAY 1 (YALE SUPPLEMENT): WRITE ABOUT SOMETHING THAT YOU LOVE TO DO.

Haunted romanticism, ravaged gaze, desperation bordering on lunacy, *Saturn Devouring His Son* first caught my attention as a bored nine-year-old wandering around a museum, and once again as a high-school student, after catching a glimpse of it in a textbook.

Because after looking at angelic frescos after more Church frescos, I could not stop myself from flipping back to the tiny printing of this unholy piece. I sought to discover the story behind it—what caused this artist to create something so raw and naked, in the age of staid royal family portraits?

I became immersed in unraveling each bit of the story, how Goya had long transitioned from a royal painter, to a harsh, but veiled critic of society, the desolation that occurred during the French occupation of Spain, the corruption of Charles IV—who was really only a puppet ruler to Godoy. I learned how kingdoms rose and fell—and rose again, how art is unafraid to capture the seditious attitudes of the common people, and how it has endured to teach us of past mistakes.

I fell in love with dissecting the messages from the past, and discovering how we still have not listened to them.

Cosette Davis

Hometown: Queens, NY

Year: First-Year

College: Davenport

Major(s): Undecided

Extracurriculars: No Closed Doors;
Groove

PROFILE

In high school, Cosette Davis was, she says, "that kid who did everything." At a small high school in Queens, New York, she was involved in almost all of the school's extracurricular offerings—from dance groups to marine biology research.

The summer before her first year, Cosette shadowed nurses at her local hospital's emergency room, where she developed a passion for biology and medicine. After arriving at Yale believing she would be a doctor, she loaded her schedule with introductory science courses. But something just did not feel right about the premed track and, in a twist of fate, Cosette ended up even less sure about what she wanted to do with her life after her first semester at Yale. For now, she is capitalizing on the resources Yale has to offer by exploring new fields, such as architecture, design, and neuroscience.

Outside of her classes, Cosette works as a case manager for No Closed Doors, a student organization that helps low-income New Haven residents apply for jobs and housing. While she loves Yale, she says she enjoys stepping out of the "Yale bubble" and engaging with New Haven residents.

Cosette also participates in Groove, a lyrical, contemporary and jazz dance group, where she choreographs performances alongside friends from her residential college.

Cosette asserts that she chose Yale because it "felt like home," arguing that among the schools she visited, Yale's student body felt the most welcoming and supportive. And, according to Cosette, her experience at Yale confirmed her instincts: On one of her first nights living at Yale, she spent a night talking to a suitemate about all their hopes and apprehensions about college. Bonding with her suitemate during their first week at Yale over their mutual excitement and nervousness surrounding the future marked the moment that Cosette realized she had found a new home.

Cosette's essays include her Common App personal statement.

ESSAY 1 (COMMON APP):
PERSONAL STATEMENT
Describe a problem you've solved or a problem you'd like to solve. It can be an intellectual challenge, a research query, an ethical dilemma—anything that is of personal importance, no matter the scale. Explain its significance to you and what steps you took or could be taken to identify a solution.

My friends may call me old-fashioned for reading a print version of *The Wave*, but I crave my weekly reminder of why I love where I live. When I flip through the newspaper's pages, I see flamboyant costume-wearers and police officers smiling together against the verdant backdrop of the annual Saint Patrick's Day Parade. I read about the progress being made in the rebuilding of houses, parks, and the boardwalk destroyed by Hurricane Sandy back in 2012. *The Wave's* myriad photos and stories effortlessly portray the unparalleled vibrancy, togetherness, and resilience of Rockaway Beach and its residents that I cherish.

The Wave also reminds me of the improvements needed in

Rockaway. As I glanced over the advertising page one day in my sophomore year, a little gray box containing the word "research" caught my eye. The Rockaway Waterfront Alliance was piloting a new internship for high school students called Environmentor, named for its focus on environmental science. Despite my preference for biomedicine, I wanted to keep an open mind. I decided to apply and was paired with a mentor who was a Ph.D. student at Brooklyn College. After finishing my first task—wading into Jamaica Bay in muddy thigh-high boots to grab slimy seaweed samples—I wondered if the program was really my ideal fit. The putrid-smelling, mosquito-infested bay was my least favorite aspect of Rockaway, and studying seaweed seemed irrelevant to daily life.

In my research, I soon uncovered a problem in Rockaway more serious than the odor of its bay: eutrophication. Eutrophication is the excessive loading of nutrients into waterways, especially through human products like chemical fertilizers and sewage. Nutrients fuel the overgrowth of algae. Algal blooms reduce the value of the bay as a tourist attraction, devastate fishing industries, and threaten public health. I was astonished to learn that the people of Rockaway, who usually exhibit great pride and concern for their community, were oblivious to the dangers of eutrophication.

Following a summer of analyzing the complex interactions within the bay ecosystem, I realized the most effective approach to decreasing the damage done to the natural world is prevention. I then pledged to foster awareness of Rockaway's environmental issues. When I finished my project, I entered as many science competitions as I possibly could to communicate my findings to a wider audience of scientific professionals. I even labored to get my work published in various peer-reviewed journals and shared those publications with friends and neighbors, urging them to spread the information.

While completing and spreading my research was a challenging undertaking, it brought great rewards. The countless hours

I spent in the lab helped me become more resourceful and independent in overcoming obstacles, while the exacting judges and editors of symposiums and journals pushed me to build my confidence and increase my impact within scientific forums. In college, I intend to continue working with individuals who share my passion for finding innovative solutions to pressing scientific problems, as I find the greatest fulfillment in making the quality of human lives better.

Today, it would be typical to see me on the new boardwalk striking up a random conversation with a stranger about nitrogen loading. I love where I live, even after discovering the grave condition of its waterways, and could not imagine living anywhere else. By shedding light on the consequences of my community's actions, I hope to encourage change and ensure my town's treasures can be enjoyed for generations to come. I know Rockaway's residents share my vision and that they will one day come together to preserve our peninsular paradise on the outskirts of New York City.

Catherine de Lacoste-Azizi

Hometown: Philadelphia, PA

Year: First-Year

College: Berkeley

Major(s): Physics & Philosophy

Extracurriculars: Something Extra a cappella; Student Tech Collaborative

PROFILE

Catherine de Lacoste-Azizi says that her high school career was disorganized but, more importantly, outspoken. A lot of her extracurricular activities involved her voice: She started a competitive speech and debate club, took part in an a cappella group, and starred in seven musicals. When she was applying for colleges, Catherine sought out a school that would provide the best platform for her voice.

At Yale, Catherine, a member of Berkeley College, is pursuing a degree in Physics & Philosophy, a joint major—and she is a member of Something Extra, an all-female a cappella group that sings a mix of pop, jazz, indie rock, and folk. She says that being part of Something Extra completely shattered her expectations because the group's culture and sense of community transcended all that she had come to expect from singing groups.

Catherine additionally works as a student developer at the Yale Student Technology Collaborative, where she designs software for the Yale community. By involving herself in many student clubs and activities, Catherine enjoys the sense of becoming part of something larger than herself.

In classes, Catherine is a loud and passionate student who isn't afraid to speak her mind. Her favorite class is Intensive Introductory Physics with Professor Charles Baltay. Though its students are mostly first-years, the course does not limit itself to classical mechanics. Instead, Baltay covers topics like quantum mechanics and general relativity, which have come to influence the way Catherine interprets and understands the world. She was also surprised to find out that her professor was one of the major figures involved in the astronomical demotion of Pluto. Learning from and building relationships with such esteemed scientists is one of Catherine's favorite parts of Yale.

Catherine's interest in the Physics & Philosophy major stems from her fascination with the hazy distinction between the two disciplines. In fact, she said she chose Yale because it was one of the very few schools that offered the major. While she didn't have an opportunity to study philosophy in high school, Catherine focused on philosophy during her first year. But she is no stranger to work in STEM: She spent the summer before her sophomore year at Yale interning at the NASA Goddard Space Flight Center in Maryland, where she worked on satellite communications software.

Catherine says that her favorite part of Yale is the friendly, open, and collaborative community—and an overwhelming sense that her fellow Yale students want to see her succeed.

Catherine's essays include her Common App personal statement.

ESSAY 1 (COMMON APP):
PERSONAL STATEMENT

I have always believed in the power of my voice. As a child, my battle roar rose above the fray, compelling the clan of four older siblings to let me have first dibs on the newest Harry Potter novel or to release my innocent American Girl doll from an impenetrable LEGO fortress. Onstage, it soared in song. In the classroom, I learned to channel my voice into debate and analysis—even when the curtain was down and the microphone switched off, I knew that I had the agency to make myself heard.

As my voice matured in all of its different forms, so too did a growing awareness that such self-expression was not guaranteed for all women. My father grew up in Afghanistan, a heritage which was my first window into the tensions of womanhood. My aunts and cousins worked as writers, doctors, and activists. They wore their headscarves with style and grace. Yet, sometimes, when a headscarf slipped, I could glimpse the bruises on an aunt's face, and my stomach turned as I wondered how she remained silent.

My understanding of womanhood continued to expand when I traveled to the SEGA School in Tanzania. There, I met Rehema, playful and bold. She was from the Masai tribe and was a victim of female genital mutilation. We bonded over a mutual knowledge of Alicia Keys lyrics and a love for chapati, the language barrier gradually dissolving as our discussions evolved beyond the everyday. Once, Rehema remarked candidly that the hardest parts of being a woman in Tanzania are that men treat her like property, and that she is not permitted to speak unless spoken to. She compared her life to the experiences described in a book she'd read: *I Am Malala*. I jolted. "You know, in Afghanistan, where my family is from, the women still live a lot like Malala." "But not in America," Rehema said earnestly, looking to me for confirmation. I opened my mouth to respond, but my voice, for once, failed me, catching in my throat.

The moment was electrifying. In Rehema's searching question, I heard the voices of my family in Afghanistan. But, I also thought of my best friend, sobbing in my arms after a boy that she called a friend sexually assaulted her. I thought of my mother, who raised five children while earning her law degree and working full time and yet was berated by strangers for breastfeeding on the train. I heard the voices of every girl I have ever known, and I was staggered by the global solidarity of women.

I swallowed. "You're right. In America, it's getting better." And I believe that it can get better, here and around the world. Unlike many, I have the right to speak for myself, and to speak on behalf of those who have been silenced. I have the education and opportunities to advocate forcefully and effectively, to speak even when Rehema cannot.

Nowadays, when I stand under the glow of the stage lights, I am conscious of the power and privilege inherent in stepping onstage. I will continue to raise my voice, not just for myself, but for all women whose voices and bodies are controlled and silenced.

Hear me roar.

Fred Ebongue

Hometown: Yaoundé, Cameroon

Year: First-Year

College: Benjamin Franklin

Major(s): Undecided

Extracurriculars: Yale African Students
Association Board; African Association
for Peace and Development

PROFILE

Hailing from Yaoundé, Cameroon, Fred Ebongue is still unsure about what he wants to study. But he has nevertheless enjoyed several focused passions at Yale.

What made Yale stand out to Fred from other schools he considered was his experience with Yale Young African Scholars, a summer program available to high school students across the African continent and taught by Yalies. The numerous African Yale students whom Fred met through the program convinced him that he would find a robust and dependable community of African students at the university.

Upon arriving at Yale, Fred became actively involved with the student body, serving on the board of the Yale African Students Association and with the African Association for Peace and Development. Through these engagements, he has kept in touch with developments and innovations across Africa. This, he says, has provided him with a sense of purpose and motivation that fuels his activities at Yale as well as his postgraduation goals.

Beyond his commitment to the African community, Fred has also persisted in his practice of golf, a personally beloved sport that has been a part of his life for many years. During high school, he even considered pursuing a professional golf career. Today, he plays with the 1701 Yale Golfing Society, which qualified for the finals of the National Club Golf Invitational for the first time this year. Fred also became a member of the First-Year Class Council during his first semester at Yale, where he worked on the Community Service Committee and coordinated a trip to Fair Haven to help renovate an abandoned plot of land into a garden.

Fred's essays include four of his Yale supplemental essays.

ESSAY 1 (YALE SUPPLEMENT): WHY DOES YALE APPEAL TO YOU?

The cultural diversity at Yale is probably what appeals the most to me. I am a very outspoken and open-minded person. I love learning about other people's cultures because I always feel that I am a global citizen. When I learn about other cultures it gives me new perspectives. These perspectives from other countries I can then use or apply in my own community and bring in a wave of positive change. In a nutshell, I feel like at Yale I will meet people from diverse backgrounds with whom I can interact to become a better person.

ESSAY 2 (YALE SUPPLEMENT): SHORT TAKES

Who or what is a source of inspiration for you?

My dad always inspires me. According to me, he is the definition of hard work; he spent ten years in various levels of higher education and got four degrees from three institutions, a feat which I want to emulate and even better.

If you could live for a day as another person, past or present, who would it be? Why?

Angela Merkel. She is the perfect prototype of what a leader should be: charismatic and imposing. Two attributes which I strive to copy.

You are teaching a Yale course. What is it called?

Leadership in Africa. In Africa, charismatic leaders are uncommon and this is a reason why our continent is falling. If people are shown how to lead then the world will follow the right path.

Most Yale freshmen live in suites of four to six students. What would you contribute to the dynamic of your suite?

Joie de vivre. I talk but also listen a lot. I crack a lot of jokes too and I am a great communicator. People around me are never moody and we can talk about anything ranging from politics to Beyoncé.

ESSAY 3 (YALE SUPPLEMENT): REFLECT ON YOUR ENGAGEMENT WITH A COMMUNITY TO WHICH YOU BELONG.

I will never forget the day I saw the smiles on these orphans' faces when they saw their gifts; it was like Christmas had arrived earlier than usual for them. I live and school in the heart of the town. From this many would assume I live in a community where everyone lives comfortably; meanwhile, just a stone's throw from my school, there is an orphanage which I pass by every day. I noticed the orphans here lived very modestly and I decided to help. I then proposed the idea of a fundraising to my three schoolmates. We were only four in our new school so I proposed we get help from the bigger school nearby. I then prepared a speech to convince the others to help then we went around their classes hoping for donations and were mostly received hostilely but persevered because we knew it was for something bigger than ourselves. The result proved us right as we brought smiles to kids who were not as lucky as us. It was the first time ever that this orphanage received donations from youths, much less from a quartet of fourteen-year-olds who left an incredible footprint in their community.

ESSAY 4 (YALE SUPPLEMENT): WRITE ABOUT SOMETHING YOU LOVE TO DO.

I love playing golf. I have done tennis, basketball, soccer, table tennis, roller-skating, swimming and martial arts but no other sport has appealed to me like golf. This sounds quite ironical considering that just yesterday I cursed during my entire round and promised never to play again because of how bad I was that day. However, the next day, today, on a cold morning and in spite of a flu, I was the first to arrive on the course. This shows how much I love the sport I guess. Golf is a source of well-being for me. When I have a golf club in hand I think of nothing, not even my swing. It is on the golf course that I express myself best and it is on the golf course that I have lived most of the best moments of my life whether it is winning my club championship three years in a row from age ten against older men or winning a professional tournament while still an amateur. Golf is like school and life in general: those who work the hardest perform the best and this is an attitude which I apply to golf, academics and life.

Meghanlata Gupta

Hometown: Ann Arbor, MI

Year: First-Year

College: Morse

Major(s): Anthropology

Extracurriculars: Native American Cultural
Center; FOCUS on New Haven

PROFILE

"It was a little overwhelming to try to capture the entirety
of my four years in one essay," Meghanlata Gupta says. Like
many students, during her high school years, Meghanlata was
extremely active within both her school and the local community. She graduated from Pioneer High School, a public
school in Ann Arbor, Michigan, where she was a part of the
student council and National Honor Society and served as a
leader in the middle-to-high school transition program. She
was also a TEDxYouth@AnnArbor speaker and onstage host,
as well as a figure-skating coach for skaters with special
needs. It was this last experience that inspired her Common
App essay.

Meghanlata explains that, when writing, she was intent on
capturing a small moment of her life that would tell a bigger story about her character. She chose to explain the challenge of coaching a nonverbal skater because it forced her to
learn more about herself and to grow. She started writing in
August and shared the first draft of her Common App essay

with family and friends in September. "I wanted the people closest to me to read it and think, 'This is you,'" she explains.

Now a sophomore, Meghanlata says she is glad she spent so much time and effort on her admissions essays. She "absolutely loves" Yale and its residential college system. She is pursuing a major in anthropology, with a possible double major in History of Science, Medicine & Public Health. At Yale, she is involved with the Native American Cultural Center, which she describes as "fabulous" and says has given her a great community and support network. She also works with FOCUS on New Haven—a first-year orientation program, in which she participated last year—and is a member of the Title IX advisory board.

But Meghanlata notes that she could have never predicted her academic and extracurricular pursuits in college as a senior in high school. She entered Yale interested in behavioral economics, but soon found that she was more enthusiastic about her Yellowstone and Global Change class in the environmental studies department. Having fostered a strong relationship with the class's professor, Susan Clark, Meghanlata became Clark's research assistant and is now authoring journal articles on wild bison and the impact the animal has on Native American culture.

"If you had told me I'd be studying wild bison last year, I would have thought you were insane," she says, laughing.

Meghanlata's essays include her Common App personal statement.

ESSAY 1 (COMMON APP):
PERSONAL STATEMENT

"Has Patricia improved this year?" The woman next to me was impatient, a mix of curiosity and concern apparent on her face. Bundled up in the unmistakable parkas and leg warmers of figure skating coaches, we stood together on the ice. Like every

Saturday morning, the rink was bustling with a frenzy of activity: skaters pulled their ponytails tighter, stretched at the side of the ice, and warmed up to practice various jumps and spins. I focused on Patricia. Gliding along the boards, she followed the pattern of her routine that I had created months earlier. With a twirl in the center of the ice, she struck her final pose: feet together, head thrown back, and arms outstretched as if to capture the stars.

I was initially apprehensive about coaching Patricia, a young woman with Down syndrome who competes on the Ann Arbor Special Olympics Figure Skating Team. Her disability has rendered her nonverbal, so she cannot understand spoken language or voice her own thoughts. In contrast, I love to talk. To say that I'm loquacious is a massive understatement; in fact, my family jokes that I could probably have a conversation with a rock. At first, my inability to talk with Patricia left me feeling robbed of tools essential to her improvement. In my mind, a successful relationship between a coach and an athlete hinged on a plethora of communication—communication that, for me, revolved around speech.

In the beginning, things did not go as well as I had hoped. During our first weeks together, Patricia and I often ended lessons at an impasse. As I became desperate to teach in the only way I knew how to, she grew increasingly frustrated with her limited understanding of my instruction. Time after time, I stepped off the ice feeling heavy from the weight of my failed attempts. Over time, as I watched Patricia enthusiastically interact with her family and other skaters on the team, I realized that the problem did not lie in what I communicated, but, rather, in the way I communicated with her. So, I decided to stop talking. I explored the various forms of nonverbal communication: body language, facial expression, and even eye contact. I replaced verbal praise with a smile and a hug. Instead of using a serious voice, I adopted a rigid stance. Even teaching choreography, an aspect of figure skating that requires intense verbal instruction, could be manipulated for better accessibility. I spent hours drawing shapes and other patterns on colored construction paper to help Patricia visualize her routine.

And it was in silence that Patricia flourished. She started skating with more ease, confident in her body and the movements she made. Because I was able to convey instructions in ways Patricia could understand and respond to, her disability was no longer a barrier to her success as a figure skater. When I watched her stand on the highest level of the podium at Traverse City's Special Olympics, I did not see a woman with Down syndrome. I saw a champion.

Before I worked with Patricia, my voice was an irreplaceable part of my life as a coach. Now, I view silence as not a gap to be filled, but as a force powerful enough to overcome challenges that sound cannot. As leaders, we are often set in our ways. We have methods that prove to work time and time again. Until they don't. To become better, to transcend the chains that bind us to certain idiosyncrasies, we must constantly refuse to settle for the familiar. For although it was talking that made me a good coach, it was when I *stopped* talking that I became a *great* coach.

As Patricia skated toward me, I told her how proud I was through a beaming smile. Turning to face the coach beside me, I said: "Patricia has improved."

I have too.

Spencer Hagaman

Hometown: Huntington Beach, CA

Year: First-Year

College: Benjamin Franklin

Major(s): Political Science

Extracurriculars: Yale Precision Marching Band

PROFILE

Spencer Hagaman applied to twenty-three colleges, but says that he is glad he ended up at Yale. Born and raised in Huntington Beach, California, he graduated from a public high school of about sixteen hundred students, where he was an International Baccalaureate student, varsity tennis captain, and student council vice president.

Despite boasting a long resume, Spencer decided to focus his Common App essay on a story completely separate from his formal list of activities. He says he wanted to demonstrate to the admissions officers that he was more than just his extracurriculars and test scores—rather, he wanted to convey his spirit. Thus, he settled on a more personal story of how he became the "guy with the flag" at his high school football games—he would sit in the front of the student section, rallying the fans and cheerleaders to root for his school's team.

Today, Spencer lives in Benjamin Franklin College and is majoring in political science. Although he has not played an instrument before, he joined the Yale Precision Marching

Band at the suggestion of his first-year counselor. He started with a cowbell and is now learning to play the bass drum. Spencer is also interested in how music affects political attitudes and is pursuing independent research on the topic.

Out of the twenty-three schools on his list, Spencer says he is sure that Yale is the best fit for him. He emphasizes how amazing the students and professors at Yale are and how much he loves to learn from his peers.

"I have friends who are accomplished composers. I have friends who've worked on political campaigns. Musicians, artists, athletes," he says, explaining that the university boasts a true "diversity of ideals and interests."

Spencer's essays include his Common App personal statement.

ESSAY 1 (COMMON APP):
PERSONAL STATEMENT

During the school day, I am an IB full diploma candidate, ASB Vice President, and the Vice Chair of the School Site Council, but at football games, I am the guy on the field in the front of the student section, rallying our fans and cheerleaders to root on our football team.

Despite my leadership roles, there are many people on campus who simply know me and refer to me as "the guy who runs with the flag." Some of those people tell me their favorite part of the games is simply to watch me sprint up and down the field multiple times and wonder how I do not fall down out of exhaustion.

Sometimes, I wonder, too, how I stay on my feet during those games. Running on four hours of sleep, and after an eight hour school day full of tests and deadlines, a Student Council Leadership meeting, and two hours of tennis conditioning and training, I am exhausted by the start of the football game. Still, I sprint forty yards in front of the fan section with a thirty-five square foot flag acting as a drag parachute and slowing me down. By the end of the third quarter, I have run a combined two miles and am ready to drop to my knees from exhaustion. Yet, I have another quarter left to run and know that I cannot quit now because the game still is not over.

My parents raised me never to quit. If one starts a task, one must finish that task, and if one faces an obstacle along the road, one must overcome it before finishing the task. However, that is not why I keep running. When I am running with the flag, I feel liberated. The mascot stitched into the flag is a mighty Seahawk, and as I imagine myself as that Seahawk, driven by passion and fire, I fly past the fan section. I don't listen to the pain in my knees or the panting coming from deep in my chest. I listen to the passion in my heart and in the fan section as we cheer our team onto victory.

I am not alone down on the field though. I have my trusty steed with me, my flag. Seven feet tall, with a fierce Seahawk stitched in cardinal and white thread on a golden background, my flag flies proudly in the wind as I run. Everyone knows not to touch the flag. I am the one who retrieves it before the game, I am the one who runs with it, and I am the one who puts it away after the game. What that flag represents is not Friday victories nor defeats but the passion and drive I carry with me every single day of my life.

That flag is going to be hanging in my dorm next fall, retired and resting from years of service. Hopefully, I will be fortunate enough to have the opportunity to bring that same drive and passion I bring every day to Ocean View High School to whichever college I attend next fall.

Roxanne Harris

Hometown: Queens, NY

Year: First-Year

College: Grace Hopper

Major(s): Computer Science; Music

Extracurriculars: Yale Precision Marching Band; Yale Rugby; Yale Undergraduate Jazz Collective; Music New Haven; Black Student Alliance at Yale; Yale Black Women's Coalition; Yale Varsity Track and Field; She Code; Cultural Connections Counselor; Yale Undergraduate Ambassador; Immersive Media Students Association at Yale

PROFILE

From the start, Roxanne Harris wanted to attend a college that could accommodate and develop her varied interests and passions. She wanted to study computer science, but was passionate about the alto saxophone. She was interested in athletics—though she opted out of being recruited for any college teams—and hoped to run track and field.

Roxanne says she wanted a combination of humanities and STEM courses, which pulled her away from applying to schools like MIT and Stanford and more in the direction of Yale. Additionally, her older brother, who graduated from Yale in 2015—in addition to both Yale Law School and Yale School of Management in 2018—encouraged her to apply.

Roxanne attended a high school in Manhattan, where she excelled both academically and also extracurricularly. A successful saxophonist and avid gamer, she's familiar with defying odds and making her mark in those predominantly male fields.

Roxanne also can't forget the invaluable help that her high school's counselor offered throughout the college application process. "They gave us a timeline of things we needed to do and followed up to make sure that everything was completed," she explains. "I applied early to Yale and was accepted, but I had completed applications for eight other schools that I didn't end up submitting."

Roxanne intended to apply to schools like Harvard, Princeton, Oxford, and Duke, but accepted her offer from Yale.

Roxanne finds her coursework challenging, yet manageable. She has continued her studies with computer science and enjoys her courses, though she admits that the rigor of the work required that she manage her time better.

At Yale, Roxanne has pursued similar interests to those she enjoyed in high school. As a first-year, she joined the Yale Precision Marching Band and Women's Rugby Team—while also volunteering to teach elementary and middle-school girls in the New Haven area about coding each week. In her sophomore year, Roxanne walked onto the track and field team and joined the Yale Virtual Reality Club.

She says that her favorite memory from her time at Yale so far has come from the Ivy League Rugby tournament. In one game, she remembers shaking off three opposing players who latched onto her during a play—a move that her coach captured on tape. She ended up being named the Most Valuable Player of the tournament, despite the fact that she had never played rugby before coming to Yale.

To Roxanne, Yale is most of all a place where she feels surrounded and stimulated by the best minds in the world.

"I love collaborating with and being a part of this community of people," she says.

Roxanne's essays include her Common App personal statement and five of her Yale supplemental essays.

ESSAY 1 (COMMON APP):
PERSONAL STATEMENT

Some students have a background, identity, interest, or talent that is so meaningful they believe their application would be incomplete without it. If this sounds like you, then please share your story.

The fine-boned eight-year-old with the exploding, kinky, palm-tree hairdo puts knuckles to her cheeks and teeters on the edge of her metal chair, transfixed. It is September 2007, and Paul Effman Music is introducing its band program to Saint Ignatius Loyola School in Manhattan. In the chilled auditorium the glorious array of brass mesmerizes her. Instinctively, she centers on the one, radically curved cone. The artist grips its neck, latches lips to its mouth, and exhales an incredible, warm sound. I was the eight-year-old, and I was the most purely ecstatic I can remember. In that moment I fell hard for the alto saxophone.

I still smile remembering my parents' initial alarm when I told them I was going to be a saxophonist. "That thing is two-thirds your size and weight!" they exclaimed. But I was sure. Their popped eyeballs when my elfin structure expelled profound sounds from my sax are indelibly etched in my mind. I became my school's first female saxophonist, and quickly its lead saxophonist. I mastered march and classical, and I fell in love with jazz, America's indigenous music.

The ancient victory symbol, the palm tree, was my emblem for success as my passions—painting, drawing, sprinting, and jazz—grew. I embraced the art of woodshedding on the sax, relentlessly practicing hard mechanics to hone my improvisational skill and sensitivity. My confidence deepened as I performed with and without accompaniment. The irrepressible sound of the alto sax became my other voice. In June 2013, I was thrilled when I auditioned for and was admitted to the selective Jazz at Lincoln Center High School Academy. This brought me, and my jazz, to a whole new level.

My life is like jazz—an ongoing experimental remix playing extemporaneously. I love the paradox of it, requiring me to pop-out yet simultaneously coalesce. Jazz mirrors how I strive to be: a free-thinking team player who walks with the crowd but with a distinct footprint.

In July 2015, I was a volunteer rebuilder in New Orleans. It was "real hot" in the shade. A familiar, intoxicating sound rising from the French Quarter wrenched me from the harrowing Katrina exhibit in the Presbytere. Never one to simply observe, I quickly descended to the stir. It was jazz. Again, jazz's defiant, uplifting, ceaselessly inventive voice drew me in.

I assumed formal black with glossy Yamaha brass—the typical Manhattan scene. But no! An unlikely trio stood in threadbare blue jeans and bright, rumpled tees jamming to the rambunctious, time-honored "Second Line." Shaded by the massive girth of a centuries-old live oak, its naturally exposed roots anchoring the fissured sidewalk, the group was incredibly captivating. Within that stark space of distressing remembrance and unscripted entertainment, I was awestruck by the electric, unified humanity.

The bassist strutted his supple fingers along nylon strings, directing time. The drummer's gray-blond dreadlocks escaped from her crocheted wrap as she masterfully beat her trap set and gifted her infectious groove. Like Charlie Parker's avatar, the alto's lithe digits calmly traversed the rapid chord changes. Ease overtook the strapping, finely tailored businessman standing next to me. When he unknotted his fuchsia tie, I was not surprised that he joined me, Converse sneakers and alligator shoes shuffling side-by-side to the carnivalesque jive. When their movement ceased, they soaked up hearty applause. Whether at world famous Dizzy's or curbside in the French Quarter, jazz offers an impartial release.

In 2016, I returned to help the birthplace of jazz continue to restore its water-damaged homes. I credit the people's spellbinding resilience to their DNA, their jazz. I am determined to spread harmony through jazz in the manner Marcus Aurelius posits: "While you have life in you, while you still can, make yourself good." I will continue to blend and solo, expound my positivity, speak with my brassy saxophone and my mind—unabashedly offering my jazz in college and beyond.

ESSAY 3 (YALE SUPPLEMENT): WHY DOES YALE APPEAL TO YOU?

Having strolled across Yale's campus many times over the past five years, I am certain I want to experience the collaborative, academic vigor present throughout Yale's halls. I want to bolster the Yale School of Music Jazz Initiative by bringing soulful jazz to Yale's residential houses. Yale's multifaceted lifestyle aligns perfectly with my multifaceted interests. I know distinct disciplines can share inexplicable connections. I want to explore the link between Computer Science, Mathematics, and Music. At Yale, I can explore my passions—jazz, art, academia, and athletics—with the confidence that I will be collaborating with the best in the world.

ESSAY 4 (YALE SUPPLEMENT): WRITE ABOUT SOMETHING THAT YOU LOVE TO DO.

I play video games whenever I take a break from academics, sketching, running, or jazz. As soon as my hands were big enough, my then nine-year-old brother stuck a PS2 controller into them. We played for countless hours, fixated on the flashing screen of the bulky, square box. Two years later, when my little brother was born, we sucked him into our gaming world as well. The Harris siblings have starkly contrasting personalities: Richard (24), stoic yet comical lawyer-in-training; Rainier (13), sassy charismatic "baby;" and Roxanne (17), busy Energizer Bunny. Gaming is our bond. Anytime we play together, it becomes a battle royal where I almost always emerge victorious (often defeating their double-teaming schemes). My agile digits also launched me to the top 1 percent on the international leaderboard of Amplitude, the action-music video game. Gaming gives me a real life edge. Years perfecting my trigger finger make me react quickly out of the starting blocks. My sharpened eyes interpret facial nuances in remarkable detail. My sensitive hearing detects the slightest shift in complex high-speed jazz chords as I keep in time with my band. Gaming dexterity is one of my recipes for success.

ESSAY 5 (YALE SUPPLEMENT): IF YOU SELECTED ONE OF THE COMPUTER SCIENCE OR ENGINEERING MAJORS, PLEASE TELL US MORE ABOUT WHAT HAS LED YOU TO AN INTEREST IN THIS FIELD OF STUDY, WHAT EXPERIENCES (IF ANY) YOU HAVE HAD IN COMPUTER SCIENCE OR ENGINEERING, AND WHAT IT IS ABOUT YALE'S PROGRAM IN THIS AREA THAT APPEALS TO YOU.

In the ninth grade, I penned an opinion essay for my school newspaper "Technology Injures the Intellect." I asserted that the growing reliance on technology—laptops, iPads, SMART boards—and the phasing out of manual writing and physical books in the classroom did nothing but stunt individual creativity. Increased dependency on technology only suppressed individual effort to stand out because it promoted group mentality. However, technology itself is not the culprit responsible for any decline in our functions—it is our interaction with it that makes us better or worse.

I think back to my first computer class in the third grade. We had to draw Frosty the Snowman with the notoriously crude "Paint" application where lines could only be drawn by the cursor of an unstable ballpoint mouse. Frustrated at my inability to perfect Frosty's hat, I dreamt of a pen that could draw directly on the screen. Back then, in 2007, that digital pen was a sci-fi fantasy. Now, in 2017, a digital pen is a reality, a commonplace phenomenon, a necessity for any successful technological product.

My initial interest in Computer Science stemmed from my hours-long video game marathons with my two brothers. I was always fascinated with the transformation of two-dimensional art concepts into full-fledged three-dimensional animation. For the longest time, my dream profession was to become a video game art designer and programmer for mega brands such as Sonic the Hedgehog, Naruto Shippuden, and Final Fantasy—much to my parents' dismay. Understanding the importance of traditional academic education and the need to earn a living, I stored that dream in the back of my mind where it became dormant throughout my middle school years.

In junior year, I enrolled in the Computer Science course and my passion came roaring back. Computer Science is like mathematics, second nature for me. As I continue to enjoy programming, my childhood dream of a career in technology is rekindled anew.

As I prepare for a college education, I am excited to finally explore the interaction between technology and creativity—Computer Science. Today, exponential technological advancements have vastly expanded the possibilities for content creation and art manipulation. With this knowledge, I am determined to revolutionize the way we interact with technology. From browsing available courses from the Yale University website, I would be thrilled to start this journey by enrolling in Introductory Graphic Design (ART 132a or b) and Fundamentals of Music Technology (MUSI 325a). Still, I see that these courses are only the tip of the iceberg of the opportunities Yale has to offer in Computer Science and beyond.

Jacqueline Hayre-Pérez

Hometown: Boston, MA

Year: First-Year

College: Ezra Stiles

Major(s): Undecided

Extracurriculars: Varsity Fencing; Refugee and Immigrant Students Education; Yale Undergraduate Legal Aid Association

PROFILE

As early as elementary school, Jacqueline Hayre-Pérez started asking questions about teachings in her church, and she was a frequent visitor to the dean's office throughout middle and high school. She recalls questioning the definition of "civilization" in her Western civilizations class on her first day of high school, contesting that war was one of its necessary characteristics.

Jacqueline comes from a multicultural and multireligious background. Her family is Puerto Rican and Punjabi, as well as both Roman Catholic and Sikh.

"I used to resent that the faculty and administrators didn't come from a point of view where they could understand my experience with racism in their classrooms and the school as a whole," she says. "I later stopped thinking with an us-them complex and realized how much of themselves they gave so that I would grow."

She gives credit for her inquisitive nature to her father, an engineer who pushed her to ask the "seven whys" and look for the root of any problem. She says her babysitter Tracy also inspired her to question misguided authority.

Jacqueline says she considers herself a free thinker.

"I was always a bit out there, and I like to think that Boston has always been a city of rebels," she said, adding that although she spent most of her life in the suburbs, she self-identifies as a Boston kid.

At Yale, Jacqueline treasures the diversity in the student body, which is made up of people from all walks of life who empower and inspire her every day. Jacqueline has maintained her sensitivity and passion for learning from others' experiences and serves as a tutor for Refugee and Immigrant Student Education and a volunteer for Yale Undergraduate Legal Aid Association.

Although Jacqueline is still undecided about her major, taking a "fascinating" natural disasters class inspired her to consider majoring in geology and geophysics. She says that the class, simply called Natural Disasters, allowed her to learn more about natural phenomena through a scientific lens. Still, she is also passionate about political science, Middle Eastern studies, and religious studies.

A walk-on member of the women's varsity fencing team, Jacqueline also enjoys hiking on Yale Outdoors trips and walking at the nearby East Rock Park. She says she values the close friendships she has made with other students at Yale.

Still, Jacqueline notes that the Yale community is not immune to dogma.

"I think this sense of 'I must be right' and 'I must be successful' really clouds people's ability to be open-minded and hear out other people," she said.

After Yale, Jacqueline hopes to attend law and divinity schools.

Jacqueline's essays include four of her Yale supplemental essays.

ESSAY 1 (YALE SUPPLEMENT): WHY DOES YALE APPEAL TO YOU?

Yale's Modern Middle East Studies (MMES) program is unique in two respects: the size of its faculty and its integration of Hebrew Studies. The faculty size increases the breadth and depth of topics taught; where one professor may emphasize the significance of tribal affiliations in society, another may emphasize the intersection of religious values and practices across coexisting ethnic groups. The Middle East is a concentration of myriad factors; its study must be taken from multiple angles. Judaism and the Jewish diaspora deeply impacted the formation of the region and geopolitics today. Yale, appropriately, includes Hebrew Studies in its program.

ESSAY 2 (YALE SUPPLEMENT): SHORT TAKES

Who or what is a source of inspiration for you?

My history teacher explains the past as a continuum informing the present. His lessons bridge the gap between a static academic understanding of civil rights and my everyday experience with prejudice.

If you could live for a day as another person, past or present, who would it be? Why?

By experiencing the day Sophie Scholl first distributed subversive leaflets, I would learn how she determined the consequences were worth the risk and how she developed her beliefs despite Nazi rule.

You are teaching a Yale course. What is it called?

"We Are All Migrants" explores how migration changes existing identity constructs, for both migrants and locals. It will cumulate into a service project emphasizing dialogue across identity groups.

Most Yale freshmen live in suites of four to six students. What would you contribute to the dynamic of your suite?

I am opinionated yet open minded and eager to learn from my suitemates and peers. I create space for open conversations where ideas are heard and respected before they are challenged or affirmed.

ESSAY 3 (YALE SUPPLEMENT): REFLECT ON YOUR ENGAGEMENT WITH A COMMUNITY TO WHICH YOU BELONG. HOW DO YOU FEEL YOU HAVE CONTRIBUTED TO THIS COMMUNITY?

I am part of Wheeler and Greylodge dormitories even though I am not a boarder. By October, new underclassmen stop asking why I stay late for dinner almost every evening, why I am on campus on Saturdays, why I help out with dorm events and participate in dorm challenges claimed by Wheeler's pink bandana. I am part of the community, helping lead community dinners, active in weekend activities, and generally around. I explain how vacuums work, help with move in, packing and unpacking, and finding things on campus. In the minutes before room checks, I help messier friends pitch laundry back into drawers and books onto shelves. I remember tidbits from overnights and listen carefully to everyday banter in the common room, bringing pieces back to Student Council and my weekly dean's meetings; even though my co-president and I are both day students, I am determined that the needs of our boarding community are heard and acted upon. More importantly, I set the example that I want and love being part of the dorms, which touches many who are looking to recreate their sense of home when they could not be farther from the families and homes they have known.

ESSAY 4 (YALE SUPPLEMENT): PLEASE REFLECT ON SOMETHING YOU WOULD LIKE US TO KNOW ABOUT YOU THAT WE MIGHT NOT LEARN FROM THE REST OF YOUR APPLICATION, OR ON SOMETHING ABOUT WHICH YOU WOULD LIKE TO SAY MORE.

I am passionate about driving change, as a student leader, active community member, and global citizen, through conversation and compromise. The Student Diversity Leadership Conference (SDLC) and Dana's Women of Color Affinity Group are spaces upholding a shared commitment to equity, social justice, and change. SDLC brought together hundreds of students representing myriad intersections of identity to discuss access and inclusion in our schools and communities. I was not the only mixed race Indian-Hispanic, practitioner of two religions, or woman of color. At the core of our discussions was a shared understanding underlying our many differences. Simultaneously, however, many students spoke from identities vastly different from mine. In all conversations, we spoke from personal experience to address a range of issues from multiple otherwise unrepresented perspectives. By contrast, Dana's affinity group sits at a single table. We are largely alone in the specifics of our individual identities; however, our underlying unity creates unprecedented opportunities for me to learn from peers of distinct backgrounds. In both spaces, I am empowered by my peers and the lessons I learn through listening across differences. I become more thoughtful and inclusive when I am both challenged and validated by my peers.

Fausto A. Hernandez Reyes Retana

Hometown: Mexico City, Mexico

Year: First-Year

College: Pierson

Major(s): Ethics, Politics & Economics; Statistics & Data Science

Extracurriculars: Baker's Dozen a cappella; Conservative Party of the Yale Political Union; Yale Mexican Student Organization; Students for Carbon Dividends; Dwight Hall Socially Responsible Investment Fund

PROFILE

Fausto Hernandez says the best way he has ever spent his money was on his electric scooter. He uses it to zoom across campus, from his statistics office hours in the Watson Center on Science Hill to a cappella rehearsal in William L. Harkness Hall. He came to Yale hoping to major in a field like computer science, statistics, or economics, given the relationship between economics' ability to describe macroscale behavior in human society and technology's capacity to empower researchers to put together the puzzle pieces of their data. Upon coming to college, however, Fausto decided that he wanted to incorporate a more normative focus into his studies, and he is now pursuing a double major in Ethics, Politics, & Economics—his first interdisciplinary major—and Statistics & Data Science, his second.

This diversity in interests is one of the many factors that drew Fausto to Yale. Students at Yale can wait until the end of their fourth semester at the university to declare a major, unlike in many international universities where students must choose their course of study right off the bat. After short stints living in London and Miami, Fausto spent most of his childhood in Mexico City, where he attended a fifteen-hundred-student K-12 British international school. At school, he says he often felt that it was easier for him to connect with his teachers than with his classmates. In the summer of 2015, he traveled to Yale's campus to attend the two-week Yale Young Global Scholars program on Politics, Law, and Economics, where he was amazed by the intellectual stimulus and social vibrancy of the environment. He immediately felt at home, which inspired him to apply to Yale and similar schools.

Once on campus, Fausto felt that all his expectations had been satisfied or exceeded. Having spent his teenage years singing in the shower, he joined the Baker's Dozen—one of Yale's many undergraduate a cappella groups—and has toured with the group across the United States. He is also a Yale College Council representative for Pierson College, as well as a member of the Conservative Party in the Yale Political Union.

But he says that the definitive experience of his time at Yale so far has been participating in the Directed Studies (DS) program, an annual year-long selective program for around one hundred first-years, which introduces them to some of the seminal texts of the Western world.

In stark contrast to his high school experience, Fausto says he was shocked by how easily he connected with other students at Yale, especially within the tight-knit international, residential college, and DS communities. When he strides through the Pierson College gates as Harkness Tower plays "Jingle Bells" on a snowy day, he feels just as struck by Yale's beauty and sense of home as he did when he first set foot on campus.

Fausto's essays include his Common App personal statement.

ESSAY 1 (COMMON APP):
PERSONAL STATEMENT

Discuss an accomplishment or event, formal or informal, that marked your transition from childhood to adulthood within your culture, community, or family.

I was walking alone on the beach for the first time.

This beach and I were old acquaintances—I had tumbled and scurried through its sands since I was five years old. It had always been a place for indulgence in simple comforts, to relax, soak in sun and water, and reflect. But as I began to walk away from the loungers, I saw children patting sand castles together and, despite feeling a pang of nostalgia, did not feel inclined to join them, and instead kept walking. Something was off. I had a new perspective.

I sauntered over to the surf, and a flashback drifted in with it, of that time when I was swimming at a competition in Acapulco Bay: I was eleven and struggled to get my bearing amidst the thrash of limbs and looming waves. I bobbed up and down, tasting salt and gasping for breath while I clawed at the sea. But then, I realized I wasn't sure of where I was going. I stopped, treaded water and stared at the finish line, in the distance amidst the wave crests.

What froze me for an instant that time wasn't the disorientation, it was my realization that I was alone in the sea, that it was up to me where I went and how I got there. I recognized how similar this walk was to then: I was the captain of my one-body ship. I wasn't following my parents across the sand, or even within their sight—they had taught me how to swim. Now, how far did I want to walk?

As I reminisced, I saw my classroom take shape around me like never before: in the vaguely sinusoidal imprint of the waves upon the shore; in the billowing breeze born from convective currents. Suddenly I overheard tourists, and it wasn't just physics. Surely the exceptionally weak Mexican peso attracted many a foreigner. I saw the humble conch and cigar vendors of Mayan descent trying desperately to sell their wares, and it saddened me to see this symbol of the inequality that pervades Mexico.

An acute pain needled my foot. Looking down, instead of a regal shell like those I would scour the beach for before, I was disappointed to find a bent straw protruding from the sand. Indeed, there were very few shells left on this beach, and very few fish in its shores. Going deeper, none swam about my legs like they used to, or thrashed how my father told us they had in his childhood. Would my children get to chase fish on this beach?

Everything, from our societies to our environment, was interconnected. Identifying a problem was easier than solving it, and on this beach, it dawned on me that one cannot tackle present and future complex challenges effectively without an understanding of the bigger picture, where science, economics/sociology and effective policy come together. My knowledge is incipient—but a grain of sand on this beach. At that moment I felt a purpose: to be an agent of change for the good, to not sit by idly. And to achieve that, I must learn. This convergence of independence, perspective and determination gave new meaning to this place. For me, that is what it means to grow up: to look beyond your immediate surroundings and expand your conscience, to recognize one's ignorance and strive to make a positive impact, tracks that shan't fade with water. It was only here on this beach that I contrasted my past and present self, and saw a change.

Perhaps adults are not those who know everything, for no one would be an adult. They are those who recognize that they must learn and act with a conscience, aware of the brevity of their lives.

By now my back was seared lobster red. It was time to go back, but it was a different me who did so.

Grace Jin

Hometown: Cary, NC

Year: First-Year

College: Pierson

Major(s): Global Affairs; Ethics, Politics & Economics

Extracurriculars: Matriculate; Y Fashion House

PROFILE

Grace Jin has what she called "one of those fairy-tale college stories." She became enamored with Yale early on in her teenage years. During her sophomore year of high school, Grace attended a debate tournament at Yale. She had participated in many tournaments in the past, and they often involved the same scene: a ridiculous amount of high-school kids transplanted onto a new college campus, struggling to find their way around.

But the students at Yale altered that formula for Grace, even as she felt intimidated taking her first steps into the storied campus.

"Yale students were even standing on Old Campus to help show us around with a map," she recalls. "They would be so overwhelmingly friendly." Grace visited Yale four more times for tournaments and tours. Every time she went back, she felt the same sense of community reiterated once again. She applied for early action to Yale and was accepted to her dream school.

Grace, now a sophomore in Pierson, is double majoring in global affairs and Ethics, Politics, & Economics. Despite the heavy course requirements of her two majors, Yale's liberal arts curriculum allowed her to explore classes from "all over the board" in her first year.

Grace went to a small suburban private school in North Carolina with only one hundred students in the graduating class, half of whom were also on the debate team. For Grace, debate was a major part of her high school life, as she spent around twenty hours a week prepping or debating. Though debate represented, Grace says, "85 percent" of what she did in high school, she decided to try out new passions at Yale.

Now Grace spends much of her time with Matriculate, a nonprofit that provides college advising for low-income, high-achieving students. Grace has also taken on a large role in Y Fashion House, a student organization that throws biannual fashion shows for undergraduates. In addition, she also works with Havenly, a branch of the Yale Refugee Project that sells refugee-produced snacks in Yale butteries (subsidized cafes in each residential college).

The switch from a full-time commitment to her high school debate team to spending time on a variety of extracurriculars contributed to what Grace called "a first-year identity crisis," where she—as do many other students transitioning into Yale—questioned how she should feel about her new identity in college.

However, one interest has stayed constant for Grace: baking. To her, baking is the "perfect mix of chaos and tranquility" and the "experimentation allows me to be creative and adventurous in a low-stakes environment."

This exploratory phase and search for new extracurriculars in college was initially scary for Grace, as so much of her high school identity had been built around debate. She explains that many students coming into college may have not yet identified their core passions, making it difficult to define the next phase of their academic career.

Although Grace now spends her time in college on an assortment of activities that conform to no uniform theme, she says that does not bother her. All that really matters, she claims, is that she finds all of her newfound activities to be interesting—and, she keeps learning about herself along the way.

Grace's essays include her Common App personal statement and three of her Yale supplemental essays.

ESSAY 1 (COMMON APP):
PERSONAL STATEMENT

Google Buzz (a short-lived, kid-friendly, Twitter-esque social-messaging platform) emerged from the depths of the Internet when I was in sixth grade, and ever since I've dabbled in the world of instant messaging. Without a cell phone to keep in touch with my middle-school friends, I had plenty of time to perfect my internet personality. The words I use, the punctuation I prefer, and the emoji I employ have transformed over the years, but one aspect of my textual appearance has remained consistent: I like to write in lowercase. Something about these subordinate symbols attracted me, and still does. When I'm asked why I prefer to never capitalize, it's difficult to give a simple answer. Maybe it's an issue of aesthetic attractiveness— my brain prefers uniform, curvy contours to large, blocky edges. I'm also an advocate for linguistic equality, and certain letters do not deserve preferential treatment in seemingly arbitrary circumstances. Lowercase letters are underestimated: they're just as powerful as a larger figure, and are often undervalued due to their size. The symbolism behind my symbols matters too, and I relate physically to a lowercase letter—small and petite, but able to pack just as powerful of a punch. My preference might be quirky or superfluous; however, these diminutive shapes have begun shaping the way I view the world.

My affinity toward lowercase is emblematic of my personality. Specificities are what I do best, perfecting facets of my life no one may ever see for my own satisfaction. Each novel I read is flagged with five different colors, and noteworthy passages are highlighted in the same color. Pink (foreshadowing), blue (symbolism), yellow (shocking details)—the system has been in place since I knew how to annotate. I've kept every case, ballot, and flow from my debate rounds in a meticulously neat file box, sorted by month and tagged with a little summary of the topic. Focusing on the minutiae allows me to perfect what I do, and truly cultivate results I can appreciate. No one may ever see those details, but I pride myself in focusing on the small things just as much as the large ones.

Using little letters also builds a pattern of simple but effective communication. I maintain that the substance of your words and actions are far more important than the embellishments, and the way I debate reflects that mentality. Often, novice debaters are surprised at the lack of "debate speak" I use during my rounds, as I limit my cases to straightforward vocabulary. Verbosity isn't necessary for efficient persuasion, and I focus on perfecting the nuances of my arguments, not inflating the jargon. Instead of convincing a judge through the flowery language that debaters often use in place of convincing facts, I make sure that my arguments do the decoration for me. By founding my style on small, clear-cut details, I can streamline my approach to build connections that last beyond just a positive first impression. Lowercase letters don't demand the spotlight; instead, their impact derives effortlessly from how meaningful, low-maintenance, and necessary they are.

As communication becomes more important to me, so do my letters. What began as a quirky habit with little characters now represents my character. By taking the time to un-embellish my text messages, I learned to concentrate on an authentic message rather than its packaging.

ESSAY 2 (YALE SUPPLEMENT): REFLECT ON YOUR ENGAGEMENT WITH A COMMUNITY TO WHICH YOU BELONG. HOW DO YOU FEEL YOU HAVE CONTRIBUTED TO THIS COMMUNITY?

As the unofficial "Team Mom" of the Cary Academy Speech and Debate team, my role is a little bit like a strict but loving mother. The 116-member team I co-captain spans all four grades, a melting pot of athletes and painters and musicians, all united by a common love for intellectual discussion. It's difficult to stay authoritative and maternal simultaneously, but I've learned to separate formal announcements from personal heart-to-hearts. My legacy to the program may be most visible through trophies and titles, but what I'll remember is far more sentimental.

Debate is often like an abridged version of real life: tumultuous, sudden, unexpected. Whether someone is fretting over the result of a round or where to grab food, I always come into every tournament prepared. Armed with portable phone batteries, excess pens, patience, and an arsenal of nutrition bars, I'm ready to help in any adversity. This motherly nature extends past the realm of tournaments into the hotel rooms and plane rides, and I try my best to create a bond through conversations with each and every one of my teammates. From the gregarious wrestler and the reserved novelist alike—they know I'm always there for a bit of mothering.

ESSAY 3 (YALE SUPPLEMENT): WRITE ABOUT SOMETHING THAT YOU LOVE TO DO.

Baking is my autonomous sensory meridian response—the quiet thud of flour hitting a bowl, the tap-tap of cracking an egg, the splash of vanilla extract—those sounds all have a therapeutic effect on my mind. In times of stress or crisis, I measure, melt and mix to manage my maladies. Like the steam erupting from freshly risen cupcakes, my problems seem to evaporate when I can divert my focus to creating a finished, delicious product. Characterized as the most finicky dessert, macarons have taught me an important lesson on mistakes: even when the end result drastically differs from the anticipated outcome, the results can still be incredibly sweet. In reality, baking demands exploration, risk-taking, and creativity, and isn't the exact science it's often seen as. Through baking I can truly experiment, combining rhubarb jam with matcha powder to create a delightful flavor. After a day of baking, I like to share my masterpieces with friends and family, eager for feedback. Taking their opinions to heart, I can reenter the kitchen, ready for my next experiment.

ESSAY 4 (YALE SUPPLEMENT): WHY DOES YALE APPEAL TO YOU?

My first visit to New Haven I attended a debate tournament on campus. I anticipated being the laughingstock of the Yalies, who watched suited high schoolers fumbling with campus maps inundate their campus. Instead, I was helped by a group of friendly students who pointed me in the right direction, even offering Atticus as a relaxation spot. Despite being completely new to New Haven, I felt right at home around students that love to share what they learn. An environment that sees obvious outsiders but welcomes them as peers, Yale exudes an intellectual yet humble ambiance that I admire.

Jake Kalodner

Hometown: South Orange, NJ

Year: First-Year

College: Jonathan Edwards

Major(s): Archaeological Studies

Extracurriculars: Magevet a cappella;
Alpha Epsilon Pi fraternity

PROFILE

Jake Kalodner's first Yale connection developed during his sophomore year at high school, when he started doing research with William Honeychurch—a professor in Yale's archaeology department. Though Jake calls it "pretty low-level stuff"—he was mostly analyzing "sherds," or shards of ceramic—it still helped him cultivate a relationship with the university. Professor Honeychurch really wanted Jake to attend Yale and even wrote him a letter of recommendation. Now a sophomore in Jonathan Edwards College, Jake majors in archaeological studies.

Jake attended a public high school in South Orange, New Jersey, with around five hundred students per grade. In high school, Jake's main extracurricular activity was robotics, a passion which he has had since sixth grade. Around that time, he watched his local high school win second place in the FIRST Technical Challenge World Championships, which, as he explains, is "a robotics competition in which small robots are constructed to run in both autonomous and driver control modes in order to complete certain tasks." Although he was too young to join the high school robotics team at the time, he and his friends started their own team. They joined other robotics competitions like VEX, and in his senior year of high school, Jake himself captained the high school robotics team at the FTC World Championships.

Jake says he realizes that there are very few places in the world that have the resources that Yale does. Going into Yale, he knew he wanted to study archaeology and is still set on that track. He worried, though, about having to choose a specific region in which he wanted to work because so many places around the world interested him. Luckily, Jake stumbled across a new branch of archaeology: the archaeological sciences, such as paleoethnobotany and osteology. By studying these fields, Jake does not have to bind himself to one region and is hoping to explore more during the rest of his time at Yale.

At Yale, Jake's main activities are singing in Magevet, a Jewish Israeli a capella group; participating in AEPi, a fraternity; and writing for the *Yale Daily News*' Weekend section. He has also taken Directed Studies (DS), which "really whupped my ass the last two semesters," he says. Now that he is moving on from DS, Jake looks forward to trying out new activities and deepening his involvement in research.

Jake's essays include three of his Yale supplemental essays.

ESSAY 1 (YALE SUPPLEMENT): WHY DOES YALE APPEAL TO YOU?

The two things I want most from college are academic rigor and breadth of study. Yale's shopping period encourages students to be curious and try out classes that may be out of their comfort zone with no academic repercussions. Clearly, Yale also has a rigorous curriculum, and I am eager to immerse myself in Yale's archaeological laboratories and it's major in Archaeological Studies—I'm already familiar with the program due to the research I am doing with Professor William Honeychurch, and I'm eager to continue my studies with him and the other members of the department.

ESSAY 2 (YALE SUPPLEMENT): WHAT IS A COMMUNITY TO WHICH YOU BELONG? REFLECT ON THE FOOTPRINT THAT YOU HAVE LEFT.

I work as a teacher's assistant at a Hebrew School that takes place at the synagogue I belong to. The idea is that, because I'm closer in age to the kids than the teacher, I may be able to control their behavior more. Currently, I'm assigned to the fourth grade class, and recently, I helped the teacher plan a trip to bring the kids to a local home for the elderly to perform for them. During the walk there, the kids were rambunctious and ill-behaved, as fourth graders tend to be, and I was worried about how the performance would go. But when they began to sing, the faces of the elderly lit up with joy. Once the performance was over, the kids sat down with some of the audience, and chatted with them. As we were leaving, one of the audience members ushered me aside to thank us. He told me that holidays were always depressing for him because his kids no longer came to visit him, but our performance had brightened his day. It may not have seemed like a big deal to the kids, or even me, but for our audience, our performance had meant everything.

ESSAY 3 (YALE SUPPLEMENT): WRITE ABOUT SOMETHING THAT YOU LOVE TO DO.

When I was in sixth grade, the robotics team at my local high school came in second in the world championships for FTC. At that age, I wasn't very involved in extracurriculars. However, something about robotics struck a chord with me. That spring, four of my friends and I formed a First Lego League (FLL) team and competed in our first competition the fall of our seventh-grade year. By eighth grade, we had moved onto the VEX robotics competition. Last year, I spent almost every single day of the season, from September to February, in my high school robotics room, and I helped craft one of the best robots that we ever built. Using a tape measure as a hook, we were able to hang our robot from the hanging bar and score points by knocking plastic pieces down ziplines. We came in fifth at the state competition, and we learned a lot about how to improve our engineering for this year. I'm back at it now, designing a robot that will shoot balls into a basket. What can I say? I'm a sucker for intellectual challenges, and robotics is one of the biggest ones I've found.

Kevin Li

Hometown: Orlando, FL

Class Year: Sophomore

College: Jonathan Edwards

Major: Molecular, Cellular &
Developmental Biology (MCDB)

Extracurriculars: Yale iGEM Competition
Team, Isaacs Lab Intern, Yale Society of Orpheus and Baccheus,
Intern for New Haven Alder in Ward 26

PROFILE

For Kevin Li, Yale is all about exploration. He is a biology major whose original plans were to major in computer science. His favorite class was an English seminar about love. He participates in STEM activities, but has also immersed himself in New Haven politics. In every way, Kevin has taken advantage of the flexibility of Yale's resources to find his place there.

Although his essay highlights his passion for creativity through the lens of computer science, he has found other ways to be innovative within his new major as well. He fostered his interest in biology by joining Yale's iGEM team, which is creating bacteria that will help break down a polymer found in plastic. He has also been doing research at the Isaacs Lab for the past year, working on developing new cellular engineering technologies.

Kevin believes that it is important for education to be "all-encompassing," which is perhaps why he made the decision to take a seminar called "Making Love" in his first year. It was outside of his comfort zone but helped him to "think critically about big ideas." He even credits it with helping him figure out what he wanted after ending a long relationship.

"Yale is the best college to find who you are and who you want to be," Li says.

He was originally drawn to Yale because of the welcoming homes that he found in the residential college system. Because he would be far away from his community in Orlando, it was important that he find a base at school.

However, Kevin found a home in other strong communities as well. One of his favorite traditions is his a capella group's Bacchanal, an annual concert where alumni return to watch and sing songs along with current members. It is one of his favorite nights of the year, and he loves seeing how much people still care about their group. Kevin hopes to leave Yale with this same sense of commitment.

Kevin's essays include one of his Yale supplemental essays.

ESSAY 1 (YALE SUPPLEMENT): IF YOU SELECTED ONE OF THE ENGINEERING MAJORS, PLEASE TELL US MORE ABOUT WHAT HAS LED YOU TO AN INTEREST IN THIS FIELD OF STUDY, WHAT EXPERIENCES (IF ANY) YOU HAVE HAD IN ENGINEERING, AND WHAT IT IS ABOUT YALE'S ENGINEERING PROGRAM THAT APPEALS TO YOU.
My childhood was one surrounded by computers, the Internet, and video games. Even the earliest memory I have of my grandmother is watching her play Super Mario Brothers on the NES and laughing as she hopped along with Mario as he jumped. This envelopment by technology drove me to wonder more and more about it. Was it simply magic that made Mario move or was it something tangible?

The constant curiosity eventually led me into the world of computer science. My journey into programming began with an introductory Python game design summer course in middle school that had me hooked at "build your own game." I still remember the excitement as I unveiled the first game I ever created: a blackjack emulator. It was a simple text-based program consisting of dialogues using user input. Looking back now, the actual structure behind that game was atrocious, but in that moment I became forever fascinated by coding.

Going into high school, I continued to look for more ways to further my passion. I began attending weekend courses for introductory C++ at the University of Central Florida, and during those classes my mind was truly blown. It was there that I saw how computer science weaved into other disciplines. For instance, it was on one afternoon during a lecture on image processing that I first applied calculus to the real world. Mathematics was brought to life using programs to teach a computer how to find edges in a digital image. Suddenly, I realized how important it would be to branch out in my education. I later joined a competitive robotics team to get experience in the hands-on construction of machines. Again, I saw the way programming connected with reality as I not only built steel arms and wheels, but also wrote code to control their movement. The necessity of being a well-rounded student has been ingrained into my perspective of education, which is why Yale's curriculum appeals to me. The strength of Yale's computer science program in Machine Learning, Cybersecurity, and Computer Music perfectly align with my views on the utility and potential of programming in the future by integrating various real world domains with computer science; in particular, I'm looking forward to taking a course in Cryptography and Computer Security. This reinforced support of interdisciplinary study coupled with computer science is what makes Yale a unique university to me. I can already see how my time with Yale will facilitate my growth as a computer scientist, engineer, and most importantly, a student who can think creatively. From working with others on GitHub to independent projects with my dad, programming has constantly been present in my life. It has been admittedly a little bittersweet to find out that no, it hasn't been magic running my devices, but in discovering all the intricate processes behind my everyday existence, it has been well worth it.

Samantha Martinelli

Hometown: Denver, CO

Year: First-Year

College: Jonathan Edwards

Major(s): History

Extracurriculars: Women's Tennis

PROFILE

Yale's student athletes strike a balance between sport and schoolwork that most would find difficult to keep. But Samantha Martinelli has been wearing the hats of the classroom and the court for some time now.

Samantha, a native of Denver, Colorado, plays on the varsity tennis team at Yale. In her first year, Samantha played number 1 for the team, finished the season on the First Team All-Ivy in both singles and doubles, earned Rookie of the Year in the Ivy League and the Northeast region, and was voted Yale's most valuable player. To her, as with so many dedicated athletes, tennis is more than just a game. The sport is not only a part of who she is, but also a source of motivation and inspiration in other spheres of her life.

What makes Samantha's life perspective unique is not her exceptional ability as a tennis player, but "the value of hard work and perseverance in order to achieve one's goals" that tennis taught her. The dual experience as a student athlete in the classroom and as a presence on the court strongly influenced her maturation into a young adult.

"Being a student as well as being a dedicated teammate [who] positively impacts the people I am surrounded with defines who I am," she says.

Samantha's high school experience involved a substantial development in her behavior and personal standards. She recounts her early years in high school as a time when she was unmotivated and lazy. In light of the person she is today, she still finds this difficult to believe.

"It wasn't until around my sophomore year that I really dedicated myself to school and became more focused," Samantha says.

Outside of the classroom, she spent her time sharpening her skills on the court while competing in tournaments. Attending a school like Yale with a strong academic reputation was not originally on her radar. Instead, Samantha wanted to be recruited to a reputable athletic school on a tennis scholarship. She was, in short, looking for a strong tennis team and a warm location. But after a friend of Samantha's decided to attend Princeton, Samantha visited her and realized that she wanted to attend school on the East Coast, at an institution with strong traditions not only on the court but in the classroom.

Danielle McNamara, Yale's women's tennis coach, recruited Samantha toward the end of her junior year of high school. Samantha's relationship with McNamara quickly flourished as she came to respect the coach's approach to Yale's tennis team.

Before confirming her matriculation to Yale, however, Samantha was considering another college. She scheduled official visits to both, but visited Yale first. Once she stepped onto campus, she said that she immediately "knew Yale was the place for [her]" and committed at the end of her trip. While Samantha recalls that the college application process was stressful, she says that Yale still exceeds her expectations every day.

"The people here are so passionate and dedicated while also being kind and humble," Samantha remarks.

At Yale, Samantha says that she has grown to appreciate learning for its own sake, rather than for a letter grade. The campus's beauty also still stands out in her eyes. She calls Yale "one of the most beautiful places I have ever been." Her favorite spot on campus is the library in her residential college, Jonathan Edwards. In her free time, she can be found with a friend at Vivi's, a popular bubble tea cafe in New Haven.

Samantha's essays include her Common App personal statement.

ESSAY 1 (COMMON APP):
PERSONAL STATEMENT
Discuss an accomplishment or event, formal or informal, that marked your transition from childhood to adulthood within your culture, community, or family.

At thirteen years old, I was pushed headfirst into the freight train that is adulthood. At this point, I had dedicated ten years of my life to being a competitive tennis player. These years of dedication lead me to becoming a top ten player in the country. My family was elated. Being a top ten player from Denver, Colorado, was next to unheard of due to the lack of elite players and coaches in the state. My family and I knew that if I was going to continue my success and hopefully play college tennis one day, I would need to leave my childhood home and seek training elsewhere. After lengthy deliberations, we decided I would be sent to the gambling capital of the world, Las Vegas.

I arrived in Las Vegas in the autumn of 2012 a completely free agent. I was randomly placed with a host family who I had never met before who set absolutely no rules or guidelines for me to live by. For a brief time, I was living the dream. No parents and no rules to live by. I was completely independent and

I couldn't have been happier. Until the brutal reality hit; I was all alone. There was no longer anyone to hold me accountable for my choices or clean up my mistakes. Those burdens now fell on me.

My life rapidly descended into chaos. The pressures of adulthood and independence had me extremely overwhelmed. All the added stresses had my tennis suffering, the opposite of what moving to Vegas was meant to do. I became a shell of who I was, riddled with anxiety and depression. I was nothing more than a frightened child who felt abandoned and alone that couldn't handle the growing pains that went along with growing up. As my dreams of college tennis began to crumble around me, I knew it was time to make a change. My parents had trusted me to come to Vegas and truly make something of myself. It was time to prove that that trust had not been misplaced.

Tennis and school became my whole life. I threw myself into training and studying with everything I had, I put the same dedication and heart into every aspect of my life. I cleaned my room, cooked my meals, and saw to all my responsibilities. With these efforts, my depression was lightened until it finally disappeared. My tennis followed and began to get better and better, eventually leading me to the number two ranking in the country and two national titles.

During this transitional time, I learned valuable lessons about adulthood. Having independence is a privilege and this privilege must not be taken lightly. In this time, I learned I owe it to myself to give every aspect of my life the attention and dedication it requires in order to succeed.

Serena Riddle

Hometown: Paradise, CA

Year: First-Year

College: Benjamin Franklin

Major(s): Mechanical Engineering

Extracurriculars: Yale Students for Christ;
Benjamin Franklin IM Volleyball Captain

PROFILE

"I never expected to feel so welcomed at Yale," says Serena Riddle. "But when I went to the first meeting for Yale Students for Christ, I felt like I had an immediate family." Even in that original encounter, Serena remembers feeling refreshed by the honesty and vulnerability she felt from people she barely knew; it was, she said, a reassurance that she'd made the right college choice. The group's weekly Bible study and discussion gave Serena her closest friends during her first year and made her feel at home.

In some ways, the challenge of being openly religious in a largely agnostic space is a familiar one for Serena, who grew up in Paradise, California. Admitting to her atheist mother that she believes in God was her "most formative experience," she says. "It challenged me a lot, telling my mom something I knew she'd be disappointed with," Serena adds. "But it showed me that I was choosing my own path and that I had the strength to do so."

And Yale has challenged Serena in ways apart from her faith. Facing deadline after academic deadline in her first semester, Serena remembers wishing she could get sick to be able to step back and relax for a while. It was a revelation, she says, to realize she could take control of her life again without coming down with the flu.

To Serena, being a part of Benjamin Franklin College's inaugural class has been an extraordinary experience. One of Yale's two new residential colleges, Benjamin Franklin College—along with Pauli Murray College—opened in 2017. The separation from Yale's Old Campus—by a seemingly vast half-mile—serves as a kind of bond for Franklin first-years, and the college itself has organized other group-building activities. For instance, Serena recalls, Franklin students were encouraged to put their own imprint on the building by painting the walls of the freshly constructed basement. Serena was inspired by her roommate's mural in the basement and will be painting her own this year. "I'm not going to be here when the [newly planted] trees are big enough to have swings on them," she says. "It's crazy to think that things we do could be passed down for hundreds of years."

Serena describes her upbringing as modest. She went to a public high school that other nearby schools termed "Hickville" due to its remote location. But a collection of idealistic teachers helped foster Serena's desire to do something that would affect more than just her immediate vicinity—in her own words, to "make the world better for a few thousand people."

Ultimately, she chose Yale because she felt that other Yalies had the same hope. Serena recalls feeling, during her visit to Yale in her senior year, that everyone she met was someone she wanted to be friends with, someone who was genuine and working toward their own dreams. "I remember thinking, 'I didn't even know people could have personalities like this,'" she says.

Serena's essays include her Common App personal statement.

ESSAY 1 (COMMON APP):
PERSONAL STATEMENT

The way fear pulsed through my chest and sent sweat pouring out of my palms would have suggested I was being held at gunpoint or standing in front of an executioner deciding my fate.

But I wasn't. I was standing before my mom, one of the sweetest people I've ever known, who has praised nearly every step I have taken on this Earth.

As she reclined in the small red living room of our duplex bathed in dying evening light, the words she spoke were muffled by thoughts running riotously through my mind. In every pause in our conversation I struggled to force the words past the rock that had manifested in my chest and was weighing down my courage—"I believe in God." Four words. That's all. But they would rupture my mother's belief that I still held the atheism we had shared as long as I'd had the thoughts to agree with her and the words to criticize the ignorance of those with faith.

Before my parents' separation when I was in fifth grade, my M.O. was to shut down anyone who promoted an idea as "unscientific" as God, and that pride kept me from understanding the perspectives I opposed. When I decided to hear the opinions of others and search out my beliefs for myself, I found myself questioning what I had been taught my entire life.

When I finally forced the words out, they slid past my lips so smoothly that I wondered what had been holding them back for so long. When they reached her ears, her eyes fell, her voice dropped, her disappointment hit me like a boulder. Did it hurt? Yes. Was I shunned for a while? Oh yeah. Breaking free from expectations that had roped me in for years was bound to get a reaction. Did all of this cripple me and send me further into isolation?

Absolutely not.

Though my mom may not have been able to see it yet, revealing my own free-thinking was worth the week of awkward silence that followed. My secrecy tainted our relationship with an unseen barrier. This raw, open honesty mixed with the empathy I'd learned to truly put into practice allowed me to forge genuine connections with my family, and later my peers, despite the inevitable and innumerable differences we had.

Embracing my individual thoughts was crucial to becoming who I am today. In the years following the divorce I'd been tossed between the vastly different worlds of my mom and dad. I rode a ship in an ever-reversing current between two lands with different rules, different beliefs, and different expectations, seasick from the weekly custody exchange. But this continual state of adaptation was the life I had grown accustomed to, and I had chosen to change it all. The words I spoke that evening didn't just declare my faith, they laid down bricks in the foundation for what would be my world, built of my own beliefs, my choices, my passions. For someone like me who had always been a people-pleaser who avoided all decision-making like the plague, this could not be more life-changing, or terrifying. But it was also the door into freedom that I hadn't imagined possible.

My situation was unbearably lonely and chaotic at times, but it forced me to build my own world. With my feet on solid ground of my own choosing I gained control of where I stepped next. I chose to question what people told me and to search relentlessly for answers, even if those answers challenged the ideas I had pridefully upheld for years. I learned how to open myself up to challenges and take unconventional paths that defied the expectations of those around me. And now I am free to blaze trails in uncharted territory where much greater opportunities await. I will never stop questioning, nor will I ever stop growing.

Katie Schlick

Hometown: Wallingford, CT

Year: First-Year

College: Silliman

Major(s): Environmental Studies

Extracurriculars: Yale Student Environmental Coalition; Project Bright; Yale Scientific Magazine; Camp Kesem; Splash & Sprout; Silliman Head of College Aide and Event Aide; Silliman Housing Committee

PROFILE

As a four-year clarinetist in a state championship-winning marching band, a set designer for shows and musicals, a member of the mock trial team, and an active player in student government and the environmental action club, Katie Schlick had an extremely rewarding time at Mark T. Sheehan High School, a public high school in Wallingford, Connecticut.

Katie believes that what got her to Yale was her willingness to challenge herself and push her normally shy self outside of her comfort zone—by trying out public speaking and involving herself in many communities in high school—despite not taking every AP class offered or being too wrapped up in boosting her GPA for college applications.

"I didn't put all my eggs in one basket and didn't rely on just academics or one extracurricular," Katie said. "I tried my best to be well-rounded and was genuinely interested in what I did. I had amazing teachers that prepared me well, and it helped to have my sister and parents guiding to make sure I sounded like me in my essays."

Katie graduated among a class of 220 students at a school where most go on to attend state schools not realizing that financial aid can often make attendance possible at otherwise out-of-reach private schools. When Katie's older sister went through the college application process, her parents also believed that Yale couldn't be a possibility, but her guidance counselor pushed her sister to give it a shot.

A few years later when Katie herself was applying to schools, she knew Yale was her top choice, having heard stories from her sister of the amazing time she'd had in New Haven.

Since arriving on campus, Katie has enjoyed exploring the Gothic architecture and finding study spots between the different courtyards and coffee shops. She counts Spring Fling and the Harvard–Yale football game as some of her favorite memories. Passionate about the environment, Katie has found inspiration from environmental conferences, incredible professors at the School of Forestry and Environmental Studies, prominent political and environmental speakers on campus, and the enthusiasm of her peers.

Katie's essays include her Common App personal statement and four of her Yale supplemental essays.

ESSAY 1 (COMMON APP):
PERSONAL STATEMENT
Some students have a background, identity, interest, or talent that is so meaningful they believe their application would be incomplete without it. If this sounds like you, then please share your story.

FACING AN ALLIGATOR
There I stood, face to face with an alligator. The sight of the reptile frightened me into a state of paralysis.

It was, in truth, a *stuffed* alligator—the emerald-green mascot of my beloved elementary school—but still we stared each other down as if confronting one another on the banks of the Amazon. My kindergarten teacher had asked that my classmates and I engage in short dialogues with the alligator to strengthen our social skills.

And I just could not do it.

Eventually, my teacher coaxed me to her desk with her sunny smile. I timidly held the conversation there, closer to the shadow of her desk and further from the army of eyes of my classmates poised at their desks, watching me.

Public speaking exercises followed me like paparazzi throughout my school career. In my sophomore year, my biology teacher assigned us the challenging Science Fair Project. I was as daunted as I was exhilarated by the prospect of leading my very own scientific research for the first time, and I chose to study the creatures which have one of the most intimate relationships with the health of our soils: worms.

I embarked on daily treks to my basement for five months to observe the status of the one thousand worms that (much to my mother's dismay) were temporarily residing there. I translated my investigation of the effect of detergents on worms into nearly fifty pages of graphs and analyses, which paved the way for me to conclude, like my favorite heroine Nancy Drew would connect evidence and a motive to a criminal, that common household cleaners infiltrating the worms' soil suffocated and thus severely incapacitated or killed them.

Seven of my peers and I were chosen to present our experiments and findings to the biology classes in a judged competition, the culmination of our many efforts.

The broader environmental issues of pollution and the impact of chemicals on our Earth—ideas at the heart of my experiment—forged the staircase up which I climbed to gain the courage to take my place behind the podium. I gazed into the audience of fellow students, teachers, and administrators who were studying my elaborate, earthen-colored trifold display as it proudly towered over me.

The voice I lacked on that day back in kindergarten slowly emerged with each breath I took as I addressed my audience and summarized the results of my research and the larger meaning behind it.

I discussed the paradox of water—how its color symbolizes purity, but how easily the everyday actions of human beings transform it into a toxic poison. Stunned, during my experiment, at the sight of shriveled-up, asphyxiated worms, I felt I had witnessed the aftermath of an environmental battlefield. While speaking, I could not disguise my dismay at the notion that each of us unknowingly pollutes when simply washing our cars and creating runoff or neglecting faulty pipes oozing soapy water—and this does not even begin to take into account industrial-level pollution of water sources. I impressed upon my peers that we cannot procrastinate solving the clean water crisis in the same way we delay lengthy homework assignments or chores—this environmental emergency calls us into combat right now.

Standing behind that podium two years ago, I discovered the power of my own voice. I planted my feet firmly onto the stage, realizing I had unearthed a passion about which I could speak confidently and ardently. It is *this* desire to better our relationship with the environment that will continue to propel my quiet voice, I hope, for a very long time.

No longer paralyzed at the thought of speaking in front of many curious eyes and ears, I scanned the audience and recognized a few kindergarten classmates whose faces, years before, had deterred me from sharing my words.

This time, I met their stares and grinned, compelling them to listen.

ESSAY 2 (YALE SUPPLEMENT): WHY DOES YALE APPEAL TO YOU?

There is an electricity in the air at Yale. Each student walks through campus with a poise, a purpose. The commitment of Yale's community to sustainability inspires me, and I would enjoy exploring the Yale Farm (and its hearth-oven-pizza Fridays!). The projects "Climate Resiliency" and "Environmental Issues of the American West" in Yale's Center for Environmental Law and Policy fascinate me because I would love studying the implementation of climate-protective measures in underdeveloped nations or defending Americans whose lands have been exploited by energy companies. Yale's wealth of research opportunities would immerse me in both my scientific and creative passions.

ESSAY 3 (YALE SUPPLEMENT): SHORT TAKES

Who or what is a source of inspiration for you?

My sister's humility, kindness, and intellect have motivated me throughout high school. She excels at what she loves—writing—but she does not let that fact hold the pen for her, and works tirelessly.

If you could live for a day as another person, past or present, who would it be? Why?

Marie Curie–she was an extraordinary, fiercely dedicated female scientist. I would love to take inspiration from her curious spirit and perseverance to succeed—even lead—in a male-dominated field.

You are teaching a Yale course. What is it called?

"It's Not You, It's Me: Humanity's Troubled Relationship with the Environment, and What We Can Do About It"

Most Yale freshmen live in suites of four to six students. What would you contribute to the dynamic of your suite?

I would look forward to being enriched by my roommates, always ready to learn about and support their passions. And as

I love baking, my roommates will come home on occasion to a smile and a cupcake!

ESSAY 4 (YALE SUPPLEMENT): REFLECT ON A TIME IN THE LAST FEW YEARS WHEN YOU FELT GENUINE EXCITEMENT LEARNING ABOUT SOMETHING.

The cold glass touched my eyelashes as I blinked, in awe of what the 400x power compound microscope magnified beneath me. My eye focused in on the minute creatures—protists, as my classmates and I had learned in the preceding class—propelling themselves with the help of long tails called flagella, "false feet" aptly referred to as pseudopods, or strange hairs named cilia. I followed the amoeba's amorphous trail through the glass of the microscope's viewing slide, intently watching it project sections of its oozing self and then scooting to that new position.

I was absolutely fascinated by these tiny organisms, even as my classmates' murmurs of disgust chorused throughout the classroom while they poked and prodded. Overwhelmed by how even the small bodies of the protists could possess such visually complex systems of motion, I loved peering through the lens and observing, like a child gazing through a kaleidoscope at the shifting geometry of form and color. Every creature on which we had spent days scribbling notes in class had come alive. I understood that I was standing in the company of one of the most basic forms of life simply existing—moving, floating—and it was humbling to pause and witness that.

ESSAY 5 (YALE SUPPLEMENT): WRITE ABOUT SOMETHING THAT YOU LOVE TO DO.

We start in the last weeks of August. Slimy with sunscreen and sweat, a hundred members of Sheehan's Marching Band swarm the turf to learn the field show. We get into the spirit of the show's theme by coordinating visual movements to the music;

we spend hours perfecting postures, step sizes, and field for-
mations; we endlessly practice music—all while sharing laughs
and forever memories with our best friends.

September hits, and I cannot deny that despite 6 a.m. wake-
ups and stacks of homework as tall as me, the beginning of
school marks the best time of year because fall means the official
start of marching band season. I wave goodbye to my Tuesdays
and Saturdays as rehearsals and competitions take over. Our
woodwind bus erupts into song as we maintain the tradition of
singing "Bohemian Rhapsody" before competing. I cannot wait
to put on the burgundy and gold uniform and march onto the
turf as the announcer asks the Marching Titans to take the field
in competition. As the drum major calls us to attention, I slide
my white-gloved fingers over the keys of my clarinet, breath-
lessly anxious, and ready. He counts off.

Proudly, I inhale air and exhale a melody.

Kaitlynn Sierra

Hometown: San Jose, CA

Year: First-Year

College: Trumbull

Major(s): Electrical Engineering &
Computer Science

Extracurriculars: Yale Precision
Marching Band; Saint Thomas More's Undergraduate Council

PROFILE

A strikingly articulate electrical engineering & computer science major, Kaitlynn Sierra hails from sunny San Jose, California. What sets her apart, in her own eyes, is her bright personality and positive attitude.

An accomplished public speaker and debater, Kaitlynn earned a reputation in high school as someone who managed to do everything. Whether she was golfing, playing the drums, acting as an ambassador for her Catholic all-girls high school, or working at her school's peer ministry, Kaitlynn excelled. She did not do much engineering work in high school, instead deciding to save that for college. Her true métier in high school, speech and debate, taught her to be personable and independent. "One thing that I really gained from speech and debate is a sense of confidence," she said. These skills have helped her in manifold ways, as a person and also as an engineer.

Kaitlynn set many goals for herself as a high school

student. At the outset, attending Yale or a similar school was a desired yet distant aspiration and by no means a certainty. "I had no idea I was going to get into Yale," she says. Hard work in the classroom and behind the lectern at tournaments motivated her. At one point in her high school career, she was known as the girl who would talk to lockers, since she would get to school early and practice her remarks in front of her locker.

Reflecting her breadth of interests, Kaitlynn is hard-pressed to pick one favorite subject in high school, finding fond memories for mathematics, history, Spanish, and English. So when it came to deciding where to attend college, Kaitlynn knew she wanted variety. "I knew I wanted to do engineering, but I also wanted a college that had a strong liberal arts background," Kaitlynn says. "Also, I wanted a campus that had a college feel." While Kaitlynn feels that she always knew deep inside that Yale was the college for her, in the end, it was Yale's residential communities, beautiful campus, and unique combination of her engineering major with a liberal arts environment that won her over.

At Yale, Kaitlynn participates in all sorts of extracurricular activities. She continues to play the drums in the Yale Precision Marching Band and is involved in Saint Thomas More's student council. She has helped out with Yale admissions outreach at high schools over the break and hosted prospective students for Bulldog Days. As a first-year representative and drummer, the band has been one of her main activities on campus. Next year, she will serve as a production manager, helping to plan the halftime shows at the Yale–Princeton game and at Fenway Park for the Yale–Harvard football game.

Altogether, Yale has exceeded Kaitlynn's expectations, offering a friendly and diverse community of individuals. This past summer, she joined the STARS program, working on a project measuring how humans put their trust into robots. In her free time, Kaitlynn enjoys marching band social activities and doing intramurals such as broomball. Around campus, her favorite spots are the Center for Engineering Innovation and Design and the Starbucks near Vanderbilt Hall. This year, she will try out rugby for the first time.

Katilynn's essays include her Common App personal statement and six of her Yale supplemental essays.

ESSAY 1 (COMMON APP):
PERSONAL STATEMENT

Some students have a background, identity, interest, or talent that is so meaningful they believe their application would be incomplete without it. If this sounds like you, then please share your story.

Nine hundred curious eyes look toward the center of the gym, peeking over chairs and gazing down from high upon the bleachers. Everyone was focused upon one sophomore student, about to present an informative speech for ten minutes about the color blue. Intrigued about how a person could say so much about a simple color during this period of time, the audience kept their ears wide open. As this student began speaking, their minds were introduced to the world of the color blue. Its origins range from its discovery with the ancient Egyptians to its association with the Danish king nicknamed Bluetooth, the man whom Bluetooth technology is named after. Blue's influence upon our culture not only involves the prevalence of the color blue amongst the works of Picasso, but also of blue's association with gender stereotypes. In all, this seemingly standard color had indeed left a profound impact on our world.

At the end of those ten minutes, I received a standing ovation. The student body and faculty of my school had loved my presentation so much, that I was no longer solely recognized by my name. From this day forward, I was given the identity of the "blue girl" due to the topic of my speech.

At first, I didn't mind. I thought it rather flattering when my school principal would say to me, "Hey, Blue!" in the hallways. But over time, I realized that the way my school community had come to identify me was similar to the way my speech and debate community had. In the speech and debate world of expository speaking, the speech event which I participate in, I am known among my fellow competitors by whatever speech topic I am presenting on for that school year. Thus, as a I freshman, I was known as the "coffee girl," followed by the "blue girl" my sophomore year. But interestingly enough, during my junior year, I was not known as the "cheating girl" (thankfully) but rather as the "bunny girl" due to the use of a bunny stuffed animal during the introduction of my speech (yes, props are allowed). Nevertheless, the tradition remains. I am branded by my speech topic every year.

Although these annual labels will haunt me until I graduate, they will truly never define me. I have to admit, my speeches did help me gain some excellent public speaking skills over the years, but my presentations on coffee or the color blue do not make me who I am. My passions, my daily actions and relationships with other people are what define my character and the person who I've become today. I love Calculus, know how to program, and am capable of soldering microcomponents onto a motherboard. On the other hand, my involvement in speech and debate has led many of my classmates to assume that I am interested in public policy or business, when in reality, my true passions involve me pursuing computer science and engineering.

Throughout this experience, I have come to realize that the rest of the world tends to function in a similar manner. People often make assumptions of others or give them labels that don't correspond with their true character. But for me, it is essential to seek the value and character within each individual in an attempt to live label free.

ESSAY 2 (YALE SUPPLEMENT): WHY DO THESE AREAS APPEAL TO YOU? (ELECTRICAL ENGINEERING & COMPUTER SCIENCE)

Ever since taking a coding camp during eighth grade, I've been attracted toward CS. Sequential pursuits with APCS and a CS class at Stanford University over the previous summer quarter only fostered my curiosity in this field. I'm baffled by the endless opportunities this discipline presents, including the fact that a computer's power and potential are dependent on the hardware and instructions we are able to give it. Because I don't know whether or not I would prefer hardware or software, I believe that EECS is the perfect match for me as it incorporates the integration of these two fields.

ESSAY 3 (YALE SUPPLEMENT): WHY DOES YALE APPEAL TO YOU?

During Yale's engineering tour, I learned how Yale truly cares about all of its undergraduates. The guides spoke of how even freshman participated in important high-tech research with professors, demonstrating how Yale supports all of its students' passions, even the newcomers. Furthermore, I admire Yale's special program of small sized seminars specifically for freshman. Some that interest me are titled "Science of Modern Technology" and "Blue." Coming from a smaller sized HS and middle school class of eleven students, I strongly value Yale's prioritization of close relationships between students and faculty for all undergraduates.

ESSAY 4 (YALE SUPPLEMENT): WHAT IS A COMMUNITY TO WHICH YOU BELONG? REFLECT ON THE FOOTPRINT THAT YOU HAVE LEFT.

Although my school does not require service hours, I am part of a community of students who live out the motto, "Not words, but deeds." Although I prioritize my education, I also value the work I've done for others. Almost every Saturday, through an organization called Teach Seniors Technology, I volunteer at my local community center to teach seniors how to use technology. Requests from seniors range from learning how to make Facebook posts, use tablets, check emails, and use Windows 10. Many of the seniors I've assisted don't have others to teach them how to use their devices or go on websites. If they do, these people easily grow impatient with the task. And for some of these seniors, the ability to connect with family members or maintain their jobs requires them to be capable of using web-based interfaces. Although I often feel as if technology just brings unnecessary hassles when it fails, society often treats seniors as unnecessary hassles when they are unable to interact with technology. I appreciate having the opportunity to assist this forgotten generation in the tech world learn how to interact with new technological developments.

ESSAY 5 (YALE SUPPLEMENT): REFLECT ON A TIME IN THE LAST FEW YEARS WHEN YOU FELT GENUINE EXCITEMENT LEARNING ABOUT SOMETHING.

Most people aren't thrilled to find out that they're attending summer school for eight weeks. However, I was ecstatic; jumping out of my seat without gaining the attention of my teacher standing across the room. With the opportunity to enroll in Programming Abstractions at Stanford University as a summer quarter high school student, I was able to continue my computer science studies after taking APCS. As I eagerly listened to the course material during lectures, I was fascinated because I learned about various processes of computational logic that I didn't even know existed. For example, I learned about Big-Oh notation, which completely changed my strategy for writing code as I started to consider its efficiency. When it came time to test these concepts I learned on homework assignments, I spent extra time completing them. This was not just because the assignments were difficult, but because I wanted to apply the newly learned concepts to the best of my abilities, attempting to make my code as neat and efficient as possible. Truth be told, I never felt like I was in school this past summer (besides on exam days) because I have never been more genuinely excited to learn about a subject.

ESSAY 6 (YALE SUPPLEMENT): SHORT TAKES

Who or what is a source of inspiration for you?

My mother; her unwavering unconditional love for me and the actions she takes because of it such as driving two hours every day to work round-trip.

If you could live for a day as another person, past or present, who would it be? Why?

Joe Thornton. He's my favorite San Jose Sharks player and I would have fun playing in a real NHL ice hockey game with a significant amount of ice time (and most likely score points through assists).

You are teaching a Yale course. What is it called?

Communication for Engineers

Most Yale freshmen live in suites of four to six students. What would you contribute to the dynamic of your suite?

As an organized person, I'd help make sure the suite never gets too messy. Also, I'd promote respect by never blasting music loudly and encouraging others to follow, primarily if others are studying.

ESSAY 7 (YALE SUPPLEMENT): IF YOU SELECTED ONE OF THE COMPUTER SCIENCE OR ENGINEERING MAJORS, PLEASE TELL US MORE ABOUT WHAT HAS LED YOU TO AN INTEREST IN THIS FIELD OF STUDY, WHAT EXPERIENCES (IF ANY) YOU HAVE HAD IN COMPUTER SCIENCE OR ENGINEERING, AND WHAT IT IS ABOUT YALE'S PROGRAM IN THIS AREA THAT APPEALS TO YOU.

My family background and exposure to educational activities at my high school have significantly increased my desire to pursue computer science and engineering. My mother's family moved to the United States when she was fifteen years old. Even though she did not speak any English, Math quickly became her favorite subject and the foundation of her career while she pursued civil engineering. Because of my mother's inclination toward mathematics, I was more exposed to the world of math and engineering throughout my childhood. Additionally, my enjoyment of courses such as APCS and AP Calculus have led me to develop an interest in engineering. To pursue this interest, I became an engineering intern at QOLSYS, a home security company, and worked on their home security panels, sensors, and alarms. Also, to build upon APCS knowledge I learned, last summer, I took a CS class at Stanford University called Programming Abstractions.

I believe that Yale's program is perfect for my interest because of its facilities, close relationships with faculty, and research opportunities. During Yale's engineering tour, I was blown away by the CEID. I was mesmerized by the CEID's accessibility to all students, including non-engineering ones. Furthermore, I was enchanted with the idea that students could work on whatever projects they desired. I plan on using the CEID to turn the technological ideas I have at Yale into a reality through the use of available 3D printers and microcontrollers.

Also, the tour guides spoke of small engineering classes, particularly with labs. They explained that Yale's intention with smaller classes is to ensure students' sufficient access to professors. I value Yale's support for its students in the classroom so that they can develop closer relationships with professors. Moreover, the tour guides mentioned that Yale highly encourages undergraduate student research. They even referred to freshman who conducted research with professors. I hope to have the opportunity to conduct research with a faculty member for an area I'm passionate about such as online privacy.

I first learned about this topic on my high school debate team when we debated the resolution: The "right to be forgotten" from internet searches ought to be a civil right. While conducting research for both sides, I learned about the complexity behind the issue of privacy and internet searches. Because of the curiosity I developed from this debate topic, I hope to conduct research with Professor Joan Feigenbaum. Professor Feigenbaum is interested in various areas of computer science, including security and privacy. In the past, she gave a talk titled "Security and Privacy in the Information Economy." Also, one of her publications titled "Privacy Engineering for Digital Rights Management Systems" discusses ways to distribute digital content so that the rights of the parties involved are protected. Her paper continues with approaches to privacy engineering through privacy audits and the Fair Information Principles. Conducting research with Professor Feigenbaum would provide me with a unique opportunity to explore the issue of privacy and security in the world of CS.

Sarah Sotomayor

Hometown: Brooklyn, NY

Year: First-Year

College: Branford

Major(s): Music

Extracurriculars: New Music Cooperative, president; Engender, policy associate; Theater

PROFILE

A musician from Brooklyn, New York, Sarah Sotomayor traveled the world performing with the Brooklyn Youth Chorus. Music not only shaped most of Sarah's high school experience, but it also shaped her goals for the future. After composing the score for her high school production of *The Tempest*, Sara realized that she wanted to become a composer.

Sarah has continued her interest in the arts at Yale as the president of New Music Cooperative, the policy associate of Engender—a student group that advocates for the coeducation of fraternities—and an avid participant in the theater scene.

For Sarah, a first-generation student from Saint Ann's School in Brooklyn Heights, applying to college was an intimidating, and demanding, experience. She began attending her arts-oriented K-12 private school in seventh grade after finishing Prep for Prep, a New York–based leadership program dedicated to preparing promising students of color for admission into some of the country's most prestigious secondary institutions. She says that the driving force in her life has always been, and continues to be, her love of music.

By the end of her senior year, Sarah faced the difficult decision of choosing where she wanted to spend the next four years of her life. At first, she was hesitant about choosing Yale. Many programs across the country had offered her a music-intensive education, all of which held great appeal for her.

"I didn't want to make a decision until I had 'that feeling,'" she recalls. "I was looking, truly, for a place to call home."

That special feeling came to her on the first day of Bulldog Days—Yale's admitted student days—after she attended an arts panel, and convinced Sarah that Yale was right for her. Entering college with a definite understanding of her passions has been hugely influential over her freshman experience.

"Yale has been exactly what I have put into it," she says. "It can be a rollercoaster. The lows are really low, but the highs are really high." At the end of the day, Sarah explains, Yale boasts a community that allows her to endure the lows and celebrate the highs—and that is what she especially cherishes.

Sarah's essays include her Common App personal statement and six of her Yale supplemental essays.

ESSAY 1 (COMMON APP):
PERSONAL STATEMENT

English is an incredibly strange language. At least that's what my mother always says. The verbs don't have different conjugations for every subject; certain words have letters tucked in amidst consonants and vowels that are silent, or that change the pronunciation completely. English was my first language, but because of my parents' complicated relationship with it, it never felt as simple as that.

As a little girl in the public school system of Brooklyn, nearly half of my friends had a parent who was an immigrant. Two of my best friends were the children of Russian immigrants; another had parents who had just moved from Haiti; one girl had moved from China with her family at the start of elementary school. So, in the background of my playdates, class parties, and drives to and from events, I heard an array of "Englishes"—there were the accents, both heavy and slight, the mispronunciations, the quirks, the strangely conjugated verbs—language truly seemed as fluid as water to me.

It wasn't until I entered private school that I really felt like there was a "right" way to speak English. My friends' innocent comments about my mother's cute accent—something I had never noticed—and jokes about words I misused or mispronounced—"Sal-mon? It's Sah-mun"—gradually began to expose me to my misconceptions about language. Speaking "well" and "with eloquence" took on an entirely new meaning for me. Anytime anyone would compliment my writing or what I said in class, I held tight to it, because eloquence seemed so crucial to be regarded as intellectual and capable of success in this country. At twelve years old, I was just starting to pick apart the differences between my lifestyle and the lifestyles of my private school friends, and from what I could understand, language was one of the big factors separating me from them.

Frustrated by the fact that the thoughts that danced through my mind were never done justice by my writing, I took to expressing myself through the studio and performance arts, especially through music. I found solace in a new language, one without concrete "rights" and "wrongs." Growing up being exposed to music that constantly broke boundaries, I was able to develop my own understanding of this universal language, and it helped me interact with the new community I had entered. I made friends through the numerous ensembles I began performing in and in the theater community. I collaborated with students and teachers, developing relationships that not only expanded my knowledge of music, but provided me with a support system as I navigated the hurdles of living what felt like a double life. I had discovered something that had given me the courage and confidence that I needed to begin stepping outside of my shell.

There isn't very much that is simple about my identity. I'm a woman-of-color, but I am also white-passing. I come from a low-income family, and live on the opposite side of Brooklyn from my school in Brooklyn Heights, where I spend my days with my wealthier peers. I understand parts of the languages I grew up hearing, but never enough to be able to fully utilize them to connect with my community, or even with my own family. But whenever I dance to a Latin beat, I feel my Puerto Rican heritage. When I pick up my accordion, I understand the pain my grandmother felt when she lost hers as a young girl growing up in 1930s Poland. Music was the missing puzzle piece that helped me make sense of my world.

ESSAY 2 (YALE SUPPLEMENT): WHY DO THESE AREAS APPEAL TO YOU? (MUSIC, PSYCHOLOGY)

I hope to incorporate music in my studies of the brain by seeing how certain timbres and wavelengths can trigger reactions, possibly tying musical ideas to releases of particular chemicals, such as endorphins for people with clinical depression, or serotonin, which would benefit people suffering from an anxiety disorder. If we can tie specific aspects of music to reactions in the brain, I believe it may be possible to develop a form of composition for psychological purposes.

ESSAY 3 (YALE SUPPLEMENT): WHY DOES YALE APPEAL TO YOU?

When I began touring schools, all the seniors told me about "the feeling"; it hits you when you step onto the campus of that one school that was just right. That is exactly what I felt when visiting Yale. In the few hours I was there, I discussed abstract art with a girl painting in the Old Campus and got a personalized tour by an enthusiastic first-year. I was struck by the energy and drive of everyone I met. There was a sense of occasion that I could not shake, and it was apparent in every person I met.

ESSAY 4 (YALE SUPPLEMENT): SHORT TAKES

Who or what is a source of inspiration for you?

As a family living off of welfare, my brothers had a very difficult youth. Unlike our other brothers, Jose broke out of that cycle by pursuing a higher education, then teaching in similar communities.

If you could live for a day as another person, past or present, who would it be? Why?

Cast as Eleanor Roosevelt in a song cycle by Jeff Beal, I have become very familiar with my counterpart, Pauli Murray. A day in this activist's shoes would recreate my perception of affecting change.

You are teaching a Yale course. What is it called?

Filling in the Gaps: The few female composers who are acknowledged in history are often known as Mendelssohn's sister or Schumann's wife. I would explore the experience and role of the female composer.

Most Yale freshmen live in suites of four to six students. What would you contribute to the dynamic of your suite?

Waking up to the smell of fresh coffee and bacon—that's what my sleepovers are known for. Cooking is a big part of my family, so my roommates can always count on good food far from home.

Buying ice cream that isn't on sale ($6.79!); writing out pages of Spanish grammar rules; opening my door late at night for someone needing a place to stay; "group mom" is my much welcomed role.

ESSAY 5 (YALE SUPPLEMENT): WHAT IS A COMMUNITY TO WHICH YOU BELONG? REFLECT ON THE FOOTPRINT THAT YOU HAVE LEFT.

I have always felt that because of the different aspects of my identity I had a foot in multiple worlds. I am a white-passing woman of color who has grown up in an area of rather low economic class. Because of the Prep for Prep program, I have spent the past 6 years at a private school with mostly white, upper-middle class kids. My experiences have helped me realize how important being in a diverse community is, and how important it is for me to actively strive to help these communities work. Saint Ann's has recently taken the initiative to support the diversity in our community, and as a multicultural student, I have made sure to help in every way I could. I utilize the complex circumstances of my life by bringing a sense of awareness to the table that I frankly regard as a privilege. While it is hard growing up feeling as though I can not mold into one part of my identity, it has put me in the position to lead discussions that draw conversation from an array of people. I have learned to become the bridge between perspectives, because diversity is so much more than what one can see with their eyes.

ESSAY 6 (YALE SUPPLEMENT): REFLECT ON A TIME IN THE LAST FEW YEARS WHEN YOU FELT GENUINE EXCITEMENT LEARNING ABOUT SOMETHING.

Since I was a child I have found myself constantly seeking logical explanations. I was never satisfied with simply being told something was true. I found myself drawn to disciplines where I was capable of finding a result by myself, thus proving I truly grasped the concept.

It wasn't until I began studying Calculus in junior year that I was able to truly grasp my capability of independence. Our teacher was determined to get the class to stop simply memo-

rizing rules and applying them through a series of identical problems; she incorporated many opportunities for us to use the
knowledge we had gained in trigonometry, geometry, and alge-
bra to form our own understanding of calculus.

I was inspired to strive to form my own understanding of
every math problem. I even remember one class when our
teacher asked us to come up with two functions that were their
own second derivative, and I had managed to come up with a
function that she had never even thought of! It was electrifying
when I realized math could be treated much like art; the process can be individual and organic, and the result completely
unique.

ESSAY 7 (YALE SUPPLEMENT): WRITE ABOUT SOMETHING THAT YOU LOVE TO DO.

There is no stone I want to leave unturned when it comes to
music. First and foremost I am a student, so being a professional
performer in the bustling city of New York has never been easy.
But my love for what I was doing inspired me to strive to juggle
my academic work with the demands of the concert season I
found myself in year after year. In a community of artists, personalities may not always click, and music rarely remains as it
initially was presented, but every concert and show has taught
me fundamental lessons about collaboration and leadership. I
have worked with many instrumentalists and composers who
inspired me to not only begin studying a variety of instruments,
but also to try my hand at composition. I have also been exposed to the inner workings of the music industry. My experiences in music have ultimately taught me what it means to be
a leader in a field that is dominated by people who don't look
like me, or come from places similar to those that I do, and
the desire to be a leader has been ingrained in all my aspirations.

Mia Tsang

Hometown: Rhinebeck, NY

Year: First-Year

College: Saybrook

Major(s): Molecular, Cellular, & Developmental Biology (MCDB)

Extracurriculars: *Broad Recognition* magazine, editor-in-chief

PROFILE

From a young age, Mia Arias Tsang knew she wanted to be a scientist and dreamed of attending the Massachusetts Institute of Technology. But during a visit to IKEA—the closest one was in New Haven—her parents convinced her to take a look at Yale.

"Walking around the school, I was so mad," Mia said. "It was making me like the school so much."

A few months later, Mia matched with Yale through Quest-Bridge, an application program that pairs high-achieving, low-income students with top universities. An acceptance letter from MIT made her pause, but after leaving the accepted students' weekend in Cambridge, Mia knew she would be in New Haven for the next four years. From the people she met during Bulldog Days to the strength of Yale's writing program, Mia was drawn to the diversity of experiences that awaited her in a liberal arts education.

Mia grew up "soaked in culture" from an Ecuadorian

mother and a Chinese-Mexican father. Hailing from Rhine-beck Senior High School in Rhinebeck, New York, Mia said her college admissions experience was not typical of public schools. Mia was part of a small graduating class of around a hundred students, most of whom chose their extracurriculars and packed their schedules with college in mind early in their high school careers.

"The college admissions atmosphere was really intense," she said. "People were doing stuff for college starting sophomore year, and that wasn't me at all."

Taking a more laid-back approach to high school, Mia didn't find her schoolwork stressful. She filled her free time raising awareness about wildlife and habitat conservation for the David Sheldrick Wildlife Trust as part of Rhinebeck's environmental club, partnering with her chemistry teacher to run experiments for a kids after-school program with the Science Club, and tapping into a different side of her interests in the Creative Writing Club.

Since arriving at Yale, Mia has continued pursuing her passions, studying antibiotic-resistant bacteria in an evolutionary biology lab and becoming editor-in-chief of *Broad Recognition*, an online feminist magazine on campus.

Her first semester exemplified the well-rounded academic experience she hoped to find at Yale. Mia balanced foundational courses in biology and chemistry for her major in Molecular, Cellular, & Developmental Biology with "1,000 Years of Love Songs" (a first-year seminar about music) and a Spanish class.

When she isn't in Saybrook College, her home away from home, Mia can be found studying in her favorite spot in New Haven, Koffee on Audubon; jamming to local indie bands at Radiohouse; or grabbing late-night Mamoun's with her friends. Her favorite thing about Yale? The gorgeous campus that first changed her mind when she was still a senior in high school.

Mia's essays include four of her Yale supplemental essays.

ESSAY 1 (QUESTBRIDGE ESSAY): TELL US ABOUT ONE OF YOUR PROUDEST ACHIEVEMENTS OR MOMENTS AND WHAT IT SAYS ABOUT YOU.

It was an afternoon in August, during the summer between my freshman and sophomore years of high school. I was about to pick up where I left off in one of my summer reading books when I heard a voice in my head say,

"I'm not going to kiss you."

Partial lines of dialogue have a habit of popping into my head whenever they want. I've been writing since I was in first grade, so I've had a lot of time to get used to this. Something was different this time, though. I closed my eyes. The speaker appeared: a seventeen-year-old boy with dark eyes and darker hair.

With him came an entire plot.

Exposition, climax, resolution. Everything all wrapped up with a neat little bow.

I scrambled to my desk and began to write. I filled an entire notebook with a rough outline in a matter of hours. It was more than enough material for a novel.

A year prior, I had participated in National Novel Writing Month. Writers attempt to write a fifty-thousand-word novel in the thirty days of November. That year, I went in blind. I hadn't really known what my story was about or where it was going. I only made it to thirty thousand words.

Now I had an entire outline. I knew exactly what I wanted to say and how I wanted to say it. So I decided to try again. This time, I vowed, I would do it. I would write a book.

I waited for November with increasing impatience. Finally, the first of the month arrived. After school that day, I ran to my computer and began to write. Every day that month I finished my homework as quickly as possible, then sat at the computer and wrote until I physically couldn't stare at the screen any longer.

There were days when I couldn't get a scene quite right, or a piece of dialogue wasn't flowing, or a character was acting, well, out of character. That frustration made me wonder, "Why can't I just take a day off?" But I knew that it would be more difficult to keep going if I stopped, so I pushed through. The word count ticked steadily higher. At last, the morning after Thanksgiving, I hit fifty thousand words. It was the hardest thing I've ever done.

Shock, satisfaction, and ecstasy rolled over me in one overwhelming wave.

I wrote a book.

It wasn't perfect. It wasn't finished. But I set out to write a book, and that's exactly what I did.

The challenge only made reaching my goal all the more rewarding. I took on a difficult task and never gave up. Even when I felt like I would never make it to fifty thousand words, I wrote on. Something deep inside me needed to tell this story, and that love and passion gave me the perseverance to finish what I started.

I wrote a book.

I will always be proud of that.

ESSAY 2 (YALE SUPPLEMENT): TELL US ABOUT A CONCEPT, THEORY, OR SUBJECT THAT HAS PIQUED YOUR INTELLECTUAL CURIOSITY. WHAT STEPS HAVE YOU TAKEN OR DO YOU WANT TO TAKE TO FURTHER EXPLORE THAT INTEREST?

In seventh grade I took my first biology class and was introduced to genetics. At first, it was difficult to wrap my head around the fact that a sequence of four chemicals joined together with sugar and phosphates holds instructions that dictate almost all of who we are. There had to be more to it than the brief explanation my teacher gave. So I did some more research on my own. I devoured Wikipedia entries, *New York Times* articles, and books from the meager science section in the school library, but my curiosity couldn't be satisfied. As soon as one question of mine was answered, another would arrive to take its place.

One day, I found a summer program offered by Cold Spring Harbor Laboratory on Long Island. Students attended one-week camps to learn more about genetics and related lab procedures. After some prodding, my mother signed me up for my first camp, "World of Enzymes." I returned every summer after that and took almost every camp they had to offer. But that didn't stop my research. I still scour the *Science Times* every week and *Nautilus* magazine every two months for news about discoveries in the field.

ESSAY 3 (YALE SUPPLEMENT): IF YOU COULD MEET A CHARACTER FROM A BOOK OR A HISTORICAL FIGURE, WHO WOULD IT BE AND WHAT WOULD YOU ASK THEM?

Rosalind Franklin is my hero. Her work with X-ray diffraction was integral to the discovery of the double-helix structure of DNA, but the fact that she was a woman working in science, a male-dominated field, in the 1950s is impressive enough. If I could ever have spoken with her, I would ask questions about her research not just on DNA structure but also on virus structure. I would also ask her what it was like to work in an environment where she was the only woman, and what advice she would give to girls who want to go into STEM. Franklin died at 37 from ovarian cancer, due to her near-constant exposure to x-rays. I know she could have done so much more if she only had time. So I would ask her where she planned to take her research on viruses, since that was what she was working on when she died. Finally, I would make sure to tell her how much she has inspired me and so many others. She never got the recognition she deserved for her incredible work when she was alive, and I wish I could tell her that today, her name is known.

ESSAY 4 (YALE SUPPLEMENT): SHORT TAKES

What are your favorite books and/or movies?

Books: *Jane Eyre, All the Light We Cannot See, Outliers, A Sense of Where You Are, The Brief Wondrous Life of Oscar Wao*

Movies: *Ruby Sparks, Frequencies, About Time, Dead Poets Society, Heathers*

What is your favorite source of inspiration?

I draw most of my inspiration from my curiosity. I'm always thinking of "What ifs" and "Whys," and my burning desire to answer them has made me unafraid to think outside of what is "conventional" in order to find a solution.

How do you spend a typical weekend?

When I'm not doing homework or babysitting, I'm either reading, working on my latest creative writing piece, or going out on day trips to Hudson, Woodstock, or New York City with my parents.

What is the compliment you have been paid that you are most proud of? Who gave you the compliment?

In 2007, we went to Ecuador to meet my ninety-seven-year-old great-grandmother. The day we left she took my face in her hands and said, "You are wise beyond your years." Coming from the wisest woman I've ever known, it meant the world.

After a challenging experience, how do you rejuvenate?

Sometimes I put on my "coffee shop" Spotify playlist (Jack Johnson, Pink Martini, Madeleine Peyroux, etc) in the background and read. Other times, I watch the Golden State Warriors games with my dad or cheesy TV with my mom.

If you could change one thing about your high school, what would it be and why?

I wish my school was more diverse. I'm one of very few people of color there, and I've always wanted to be able to talk to people who can identify with the experiences I've had as a minority.

What would you contribute to your future college campus community?

I love writing, so I would definitely get involved with literary magazines and newspapers on campus. I would also join community outreach groups, particularly those that focus on Hispanic empowerment.

Lillian Yuan

Hometown: Naperville, IL
Year: First-Year
College: Pierson
Major(s): Cognitive Science; Economics
Extracurriculars: Steppin' Out;
Hippopotamus Literary Magazine, editor;
Matriculate; Asian American Cultural Center,
peer liaison

PROFILE

Lillian Yuan is a sophomore in Pierson College from Naperville, Illinois, a suburb of Chicago. Back home, she and her twin sister, Vivian, were affectionately known as "the power twins" because of their involvement with school activities. In the classroom, Lillian was particularly interested in English, which led her to write for the school's literary magazine. Meanwhile, outside the classroom, she spent time as president of DECA, a business club focused on community outreach, and sang in her school's show choir.

When looking for college options, Lillian wanted to find a place where she could feel comfortable exploring new fields without having to sacrifice her other interests. She was not sure whether she wanted to pursue English further and wanted to try other disciplines like economics and cognitive science.

Yale appeared to be a perfect fit, with a competitive

academic environment that also allowed for intellectual exploration. Before arriving for her first year, Lillian, while incredibly excited to attend, was worried the other members of her incoming class might be "intimidatingly competitive" or "too smart." However, after spending her first year at Yale, she quickly came to realize that while her classmates were indeed impressive, the caliber of her fellow Yalies pushed her to grow as both a person and a student.

At Yale, Lillian has continued to pursue a broad array of activities. She not only works to fight against the underrepresentation of Asians in national politics but also performs on Yale's step team, Steppin' Out, and writes for *Hippopotamus Literary Magazine*, a new publication that she helped create. She also works for Matriculate—an organization that matches current undergraduate mentors to promising low-income high school students—and is active in Yale Students for Christ. Lillian is often found on the Divinity School campus, a short walk north of the center of undergraduate life, working on her assignments in cognitive science and economics.

Lillian's essays include her Common App personal statement and three of her Yale supplemental essays.

ESSAY 1 (COMMON APP):
PERSONAL STATEMENT

For as long as I can remember, my twin sister and I have communicated through song lyrics. Our shared playlist thrums through my earbuds as I sit on the plane, watching the clouds roll out and a beautiful college campus roll in. It reminds me of how much we've grown with and learned from each other, of how much of my personal identity has come from the one we share. So I close my eyes and just listen.

"We'll sit in our bedrooms and read aloud, like a passage from goodnight moon . . ." - Track 1: Goodnight Moon

When Vivian finally closes her Calculus textbook, I crack open a very different kind of book. She groans.

"Please?" I say. "Just one chapter. I promise."

With a sigh, she moves over on the twin bed. I give a squeal of delight, plunging right in with my best character voices. Every couple pages, I insert the word "banana" into a sentence to make sure Vivian is still listening, but now she's wide awake. One chapter spirals into three to five, and one night of pulling a Benjamin Buttons and becoming fearless, overly zealous children turns into a tradition. As we laugh, cry, and push the boundaries of imagination together, I decide that this is what life should be about: dreaming large and loving larger.

"You raise me up, so I can stand on mountains . . ." - Track 2: You Raise Me Up

My breath comes out in sporadic puffs. This is it, I think. I've finally found the one thing I can't conquer with hard work, optimism, and willpower: the mile.

Vivian strides a couple paces in front, but she slows down and reaches a hand out. She tugs on my arm and yells encouragements through her own exhaustion, so I pick up my pace and forge through, sprinting the last 150 meters by her side.

When blood starts flowing normally to my brain again, I think about all the ways we challenge each other through our competitive natures inherent to being twins. But even though our competition pushes me to be better, our unwavering support for each other pushes me to be the best that I can be—as an athlete, a student, and ultimately a person.

"Come on let it go, just let it be, why don't you be you and I'll be me?" - Track 3: Let It Go

Connor looks at us skeptically.

"I swear we're fraternal," I repeat.

"But you guys are basically the same person," he says, baffled.

Before high school, a comment like that would've punched a hole in my self-esteem. But I realized that being so similar to someone else molded my individuality in incredible, ironic ways, every joke about my replaceability fueling my drive to distinguish myself. I learned to define myself both inside the context of being a twin, balancing Vivian's strict rationality with my more emotional, philosophical musings, and outside of it, finding a family and new identity in a Christian community and delving deep into creative writing, social work, and other passions unique to me.

So now I just laugh. "If you don't believe me," I joke, "you can just ask my mom for the birth certificate."

"I don't know if I've been changed for the better, but because I knew you, I have been changed for good." - Track 4: For Good

My favorite duet from the musical "Wicked" plays me into the landing gate, where so many new songs await. As I hum along to this one, I tell Vivian all that I need to say: that our timeless traditions have shaped my creativity, spontaneity, and sheer love of living; that her unconditional support pushes me to improve myself ceaselessly and conquer the unconquerable; that this shared identity has paved the way for me to build my own.

That being a twin has changed me, for good.

ESSAY 2 (YALE SUPPLEMENT): WHY DOES YALE APPEAL TO YOU?

Ever since I read Leigh Bardugo's *Six of Crows* and watched Sam Tsui's debut performance in Yale's hilarious music video, I've dreamed of attending the college that shaped such inspirational figures in my life. Now my reasons are less star-struck: I long to experience Yale's equally vibrant musical, academic, and social scenes, to class-hop during Yale's shopping period, to participate in the rigorous Directed Studies program. I long to forge lifelong relationships in one of the twelve tight-knit residential colleges while networking in the large, research-oriented university. I long to become an inspirational figure myself; that's why *I* choose Yale.

ESSAY 3 (YALE SUPPLEMENT): REFLECT ON A TIME IN THE LAST FEW YEARS WHEN YOU FELT GENUINE EXCITEMENT LEARNING ABOUT SOMETHING.

What is the ethical dilemma that rises from memory hacking? How else can memory be distorted? Is memory meant to be accurate or adaptive?

My eyes were glued to the screen, but my mind was chugging away. NOVA's *Memory Hackers,* a documentary recommended to me by a friend, had me completely enthralled. The idea that something so intrinsic to the human experience could be so complex fascinated me to no end, and I needed to learn more.

A month later, I began to tackle all my questions through a Humanities Capstone. I started my school days with visits to the library, my pile of articles from the local community college and various databases growing along with my enthusiasm. I poured over study upon study discussing memory distortion through false memory implantation, collective memory formation, radical museology, and optogenetics, scribbling notes clandestinely during lulls in my other classes. Though I was searching for support for my thesis—that memory's malleability can help us develop historical consciousness and sense of self—I found something more valuable along the way: a budding interest in not only cognitive sciences but independent research, one that will stay with me wherever I go.

ESSAY 4 (YALE SUPPLEMENT): WRITE ABOUT SOMETHING THAT YOU LOVE TO DO.

Three sentences in. No backspace button—just scratch away the words. Relish in the ink smoothing out your thoughts. Create a Kaz Brekker, a boy with a hardened heart that cheats life and was cheated by life, or a Skeeter Phelan who stops at nothing in her pursuit of truth. Let the words run you over with their power and, more often than not, clumsiness. It doesn't matter—just go.

In moments like these, creative writing takes over my heart and mind. My mother's calls to eat dinner don't exist, and three hours squeeze into just three minutes of intense dialogue. My assignment notebook transforms into a series of letters never sent. The library's Georgia Pacific–brand bathroom amenities become poetic metaphors for pushing past constructed horizons while I push my own.

Throughout my life, from writing a fifth-grade free verse about ostriches to grueling over a National Novel Writing Month story to running a book blog with four enthusiastic readers and best friends, my passion for creative writing has continuously evolved. What started as fun turned to catharsis, and now, to inspiration: inspiration to think deeply, live wholeheartedly, and appreciate the beauty in every small moment.

Alec Zbornak

Hometown: Los Angeles, CA

Year: First-Year

College: Ezra Stiles

Major(s): Humanities

Extracurriculars: Just Add Water; *The Yale Record*, writer

PROFILE

Alec is a rising sophomore in Ezra Stiles College, originally hailing from Los Angeles. Although Alec is majoring in humanities, he also has taken a keen interest in East Asian languages and literature while at Yale, an interest that prompted him to spend his summer in Beijing, China, after his first year of college, participating in an immersive language program in Chinese language and culture.

Before coming to Yale, Alec was engaged in a wide variety of extracurricular activities. He captained his school's speech and debate team and was an editor for the school newspaper, joined student council, and coached special Olympics, specifically for track and soccer. However, since coming to Yale, Alec decided to branch out and explore new activities and communities. He still maintains some of his passions, such as writing, by contributing to *The Record*. He also codirected and cowrote a play for the Yale Children's Theater.

Beyond this, he is a member of Just Add Water, an improv group that, according to Alec, has provided him with one of the most important communities he has found at Yale. It was this very sense that drew him to Yale in the first place: Upon researching and asking about Yale, Alec thought it would be the place where he would find the most welcoming, friendly, and accepting group of people.

On a snow day, Alec was walking around campus; he marveled at the snow and caught snowflakes with his tongue. Eventually he turned around and saw another student walking across campus doing the exact same thing. It was this memory that best exemplified what he loves about his community: people at Yale are driven, impressive and intelligent, but they are also fun and silly and rarely take themselves too seriously.

Alec's essays include five of his Yale supplemental essays.

ESSAY 1 (YALE SUPPLEMENT): WHY DO THESE AREAS APPEAL TO YOU? (POLITICAL SCIENCE, HUMANITIES, ETHICS, PHILOSOPHY)

My intense love for humanity has led me to pursue these areas of academic exploration. While I acknowledge that humankind is in no way perfect, when I look to our extensive history, I can't help but feel overwhelmed and amazed by what we have accomplished. Whether it's discovering the most effective way to lead and organize society, the philosophical roots behind our impulses and actions, or the ways in which the human condition has been artistically and historically expressed, I want to study humanity from multiple angles so that I can get the most complete understanding possible.

ESSAY 2 (YALE SUPPLEMENT): WHY DOES YALE APPEAL TO YOU?

In addition to the focus on a well-rounded liberal arts education, the ability to "shop" around for classes that interest me, and the impressive access to research opportunities, I love Yale because of the strong sense of community that it fosters. Yale's ability to bring together amazing students from around the world, while encouraging collaboration and teamwork is impressive and creates the supportive learning environment that I crave. Additionally, the inter-residential-college competitions seem fun and exciting, and I would love the opportunity to grow even closer to my classmates while competing in the Freshman Olympics.

ESSAY 3 (YALE SUPPLEMENT): SHORT TAKES

Who or what is a source of inspiration for you?

I admire my mom because of her ability to make others feel genuinely loved and appreciated. It's impossible to have a conversation with her without smiling.

If you could live for a day as another person, past or present, who would it be? Why?

I would live as Neal Cassidy during the counter-culture period, so that I could be a part of the Beat movement and fight for passion, self-expression, and love.

You are teaching a Yale course. What is it called?

I am teaching "Imagineering: How to Dream like Disney," a course detailing the intersection of creative thinking and dream chasing, and how those philosophies can be applied to everyday life.

Most Yale freshmen live in suites of four to six students. What would you contribute to the dynamic of your suite?

In addition to my light-hearted sense of humor, I believe that I could use my skills in photography to take awesome portraits of my suite mates, which we could use to decorate our room.

ESSAY 4 (YALE SUPPLEMENT): WHAT IS A COMMUNITY TO WHICH YOU BELONG? REFLECT ON THE FOOTPRINT THAT YOU HAVE LEFT.

Since I was fourteen years old, I have volunteered every Saturday morning to coach soccer and track and field for the Special Olympics. For the past five years, I have worked closely with the same group of special needs athletes and have developed personal relationships with each one. The pure love, affection, and unadulterated innocence that they radiate are infectious and propel me to be a kinder and more compassionate person. Grateful for this eye-opening experience, I wanted to share it with my classmates and get my school community involved with the program. As the president of the Community Service Leadership Team, I worked extensively with the administration to organize and lead a sports skills clinic on campus for special needs athletes across the district, as well as a school-wide End-the-R-Word campaign to promote a respect for and understanding of people with special needs. Whenever I walk by the commemorative banner hanging in Loyola's hallway and see the hundreds of signatures of students pledging their respect, knowing that I made a difference in my school community, I smile widely, almost as widely as when Mark, one of my soccer players, calls me his "best buddy."

ESSAY 5 (YALE SUPPLEMENT): REFLECT ON A TIME IN THE LAST FEW YEARS WHEN YOU FELT GENUINE EXCITEMENT LEARNING ABOUT SOMETHING.

AP English Language was the best class that I have ever taken, because we went beyond the requirements needed for the AP test and studied literature intensely. We made bold connections to philosophy, critical theory, and history. From Christian readings of *Beowulf* to post-colonial analyses of *Heart of Darkness*, we always found ways to look at texts from different perspectives. I distinctly remember the feeling of excited anticipation that I had before each class and the sense of amazed wonder that I felt at the end. Through this course, I truly found my love for the humanities. My efforts culminated in an eleven-page research paper, exploring how Shakespeare's *Macbeth* presents the nuanced strata of Elizabethan ontology influenced simultaneously by its existing religious foundation and the rise of scientific empiricism. For one month I researched the topic intensively and met constantly with my teacher; I even contacted a university professor and conducted a personal interview with him. That paper had been the hardest I had ever worked on a single assignment, but it was all worth it because it gave me the opportunity to develop a newfound sense of scholarly passion, curiosity, and drive.

Emma*

PROFILE

Emma, who hails from a small town in the American South, followed a very different path from most of her high school classmates. In fact, about a fifth of her class dropped out before their graduation—and many of those who did graduate did not go on to college.

Nevertheless, Emma was determined to find an educational environment that would challenge her. She applied to college through QuestBridge—a nonprofit program that seeks to match motivated students from disadvantaged backgrounds to selective schools with robust financial aid packages. She was selected as a QuestBridge Finalist, and although she did not match with Yale, she received a "likely" letter, a letter sent to a small portion of the regular-decision applicant pool prior to the official March decision date, signifying that they are "likely" to be accepted.

In the college search process, Emma focused on small liberal arts colleges, hoping to major in English. Although Yale is bigger than many of the other schools she applied to, Emma felt encouraged by the idea of the residential college system. At first, Yale presented a series of difficult adjustments: the rigorous classes, the cold climate, and the urban environment, to name a few. But Emma was thrilled to finally

---

*We have changed Emma's name to protect the privacy of other individuals described in her essay.

be around other students who were engaged and enthusiastic about learning.

For Emma, the best part of Yale so far has been the community provided by her residential college. She remarks that she was surprised by how accepting and understanding her classmates were in spite of the sometimes staggering differences in their backgrounds. She's also loved the quirky residential college traditions, such as the annual water-gun fight, in which the college's first-years try to invade its courtyard from Old Campus while the older students defend it.

Outside of her classwork and engagement with residential life, Emma works fifteen hours a week through Yale's work-study program. She also volunteers with New Haven REACH, a student-run organization that helps New Haven youth access higher education, and Matriculate, a national nonprofit that partners college students with low-income, high-achieving high schoolers to provide college admissions advice. Through these organizations, Emma hopes she can give other high schoolers the chance to access the same kinds of opportunities that she herself has found.

Emma's essays include her Common App personal statement and her QuestBridge essay.

ESSAY 1 (COMMON APP):
PERSONAL STATEMENT

If I could write a letter to myself one year ago, when I faced one of the most difficult transitional periods of my life, it would start like this: "Dear Emma" . . . I would skip a line and mark so many others out as I try to put into words what I went through and how exactly I came out on top.

To understand my metamorphosis to adulthood, first imagine growing up in my Southern household: all the men are alcoholics; all the women never leave the men, no matter what. I was expected to get a boyfriend and eventually marry him, the sooner out of high school the better. Education and feminism were not valued. The women cooked. The women cleaned.

My dad was probably worse than the others. The youngest child and physically disabled, he led a hard life that he's never handled well. I think the longest period he's went without drugs or alcohol is a month. He lives off disability and he always married a new woman to take care of him, after the old one got tired of it.

Now imagine possessing some above average intelligence that I got from my crazy, bipolar mother (my father's words, not mine). Imagine living in a house where a NASCAR race or a new TV show was more important than homework; imagine wishing for a private bathroom and kitchen so you never had to leave your room and interact with your family.

Now imagine it's your sixteenth birthday. Your father is in between wives and at the races on this day because he figured you wouldn't mind. You honestly don't. Your mother keeps saying her door is always open if you ever wanted to leave it all.

Imagine you take the jump. You move out while your father is away. He pulls in as you're leaving with the last of your belongings. He realizes what is happening and he screams, "How am I supposed to survive without your Social Security check?" Not "I love you." Not "Don't go." Just "I only need you for money."

You hope you made the right decision, yet in your new home, it is anything but easy. You struggle with your mother to live off $1,200 until your check is transferred over to her; you put up with her bipolar moods and the seemingly constant guilt from leaving your father. You are reminded of this sporadically, as a relative calls you a thief, as your father threatens to turn you in to the police for taking your personal belongings.

The stress from all this was unbearable. I could not stand to be happy with my mother as I wondered how I could leave my father when he needed me to take care of him.

Yet, if there was one thing I would say to myself a year ago, it would be that everything turns out alright. Life goes on. Making the decision to uproot yourself so you can grow in healthier soil is never easy, but as you blossom, as you grow, you soon realize the decision was the right one and that everything will eventually work out for the best.

That day, on my sixteenth birthday, I not only changed in age, but I also changed in character. No longer was I going to allow someone to use me for his gain; no longer was I going to stand idly by as my life was poured down the drain and replaced with an empty beer bottle. That day, I made the decision to become my own person and to do what's best for me, for my life, for my education. I transformed from a person to be used into one who would not be tamed. I made my life my own, and I knew then that it would never be the same.

ESSAY 2: QUESTBRIDGE ESSAY

We are interested in learning more about you and the context in which you have grown up, formed your aspirations, and accomplished your academic successes. Please describe the factors and challenges that have most shaped your personal life and aspirations. How have these factors helped you grow?

I was a child without a future, a girl without a name, a person without a drive. Now, I am none of these things. I used to simply exist, but now I am getting ready to live and to leave my mark upon the world, a world that had never noticed me until I gave it a reason to.

I was born into this world to parents who divorced before I was even a year old. My father is physically handicapped: he attempts to make up for his lack of legs with the sheer amount of alcohol he regularly consumes. My mother suffers from bipolar disorder: her manias and depression force her and me to ride a rollercoaster of emotions. Both of my parents receive Social Security checks for their disabilities, and that is how we have survived my entire life: living paycheck to paycheck and hoping it all worked out, yet never applying pressure or willpower to shape our existence into something more.

For the longest time, I believed that such a family situation was normal: every child had as much family responsibility—doing all the cooking and cleaning by age eleven after my father divorced my first stepmother; every dad drank and belittled every kid's mother when she wasn't around; every time a child asked for new clothes, she was told there wasn't enough money even as two thirty packs sat cooling in the fridge. For the longest time, I never realized the childhood I had experienced was anything but the regular American upbringing. Transferring to a larger school system in eighth grade, expanding my knowledge through a better education, and being exposed to a wide array of books and other types of lives revealed to me that the family I had, the childhood I had experienced, was anything but normal.

Being raised in a household when one has to force her parents to help her study for a first grade spelling test does not influence a child to strive to become smarter. It was my own drive and need for shelter from my life that led me to read books deep into the night, as my dad screamed louder and louder at the TV. It was my own intelligence that had my new school teachers asking me to move up to more advanced math and science classes despite the fact that I didn't believe I was capable. It was my own search for knowledge and understanding that led me to the truth about my life and revealed to me the pit of my existence alongside the ladder of education by which I could escape it.

By freshman year, with no encouragement from my father (with whom I lived at the time), I decided to finally push myself and see if I was capable of taking all advanced classes. In these advanced classes, however, I was not just capable: I excelled at them, and by the end of the first semester of high school, I was ranked number one out of three hundred students. Nearly all of my grades were a hundred and it became a personal goal of mine to see how many times I could have one hundreds across my report card. By sophomore year, I joined UIL, an academic competition where I was finally able to stretch the wings of my mind and write the thoughts I had never been greatly encouraged to express.

In the summer preceding my junior year, I finally moved out of my father's unstable home and into my mother's more tolerable one. We now struggle to live off of her and my Social Security checks. When I left my father's house, he was angry about the loss of my check, but not the loss of his daughter. He now contacts me only on holidays. Yet, despite the stress of my living and financial situations, I have managed to keep a firm grasp on my valedictorian rank and excel at the extracurricular and work activities that I simultaneously balance.

When a person is her own greatest motivation, she can accomplish almost anything. Despite her background and childhood, with a determination and an education, any person can become anything. After taking seventeen years to realize this, I have finally found the path of achievement that I will continue down, the path that I will follow for the rest of my life. With a solid education and firm self-resolve, I now know I am capable of breaking the cycle of my family and beginning a positive one of my own. I am not doing this for anyone else: I'm doing it for me, for the girl who once had no future, no drive, and no name.

Sophomores

Madeline Bender

Hometown: New York City, NY

Year: Sophomore

College: Timothy Dwight

Major(s): Ecology & Evolutionary Biology; Classics

Extracurriculars: *Yale Daily News*, *SciTech* editor; Yale Concert Band

PROFILE

Maddie Bender, a New York City native, describes her high school self as a "jack of all trades." Inside the classroom, she especially loved science and Latin; outside of it, she dabbled in a remarkably wide range of activities over the course of her four years, from writing for school publications and leading the Science Olympiad to participating in three varsity sports—tennis, skiing, and softball—and playing principal clarinet for her high school's concert band.

It was this mix of interests that attracted her to Yale: a university that, to her, epitomized the appeal of the liberal arts. She was drawn simultaneously to the University's Classics department, its student-run daily newspaper—the *Yale Daily News*—and its strong biology and life sciences departments. Yale's a-little-bit-of-everything philosophy, which already resonated strongly with Maddie, seemed perfectly exemplified by her tour guide, a cognitive science major who was, like Maddie, also interested in writing.

Sure enough, since the start of her college experience,

Maddie has involved herself in almost all of the aspects that originally attracted her to the University. She is double-majoring in Ecology & Evolutionary Biology and classics, has been a science and technology editor at the *News*, plays the clarinet for the Yale Concert Band, and is a member of the club tennis team.

That she mentioned almost all of these activities on her Yale application is a testament to Maddie's unusually clear vision for herself. In fact, unlike the vast majority of students, Maddie even knew when she applied which classes she wanted to take: In a supplemental essay for Yale, Maddie mentioned a course called Roman Dining, which she then enrolled in during the fall of her sophomore year. She enjoyed it just as much as she thought she would—in fact, she maintains, it was one of her two favorite courses that she's taken so far.

Even though Maddie fulfills a variety of roles on campus, she works hard to ensure there's a balance—she safeguards time for relaxing with friends, partaking in Yale traditions, and getting to know New Haven better. A fan of Arethusa Farm Dairy's ice cream, she names Frank Pepe's Pizzeria Napoletana and Modern Apizza as her two favorite New Haven pizzerias. She especially loves spending time among the tight-knit community of her residential college, Timothy Dwight.

Maddie's essays include her Common App personal statement and four Yale supplemental essays.

ESSAY 1 (COMMON APP):
PERSONAL STATEMENT

"Isn't Latin a dead language?" my friends would ask. "Not if you follow the Pope on Twitter!" I'd retort.

Still, even in 140-character increments, translation did not come easily to me. At first, I had difficulty comprehending basic sentence structures. Then, three years later, I found myself reading Cicero and Pliny. Almost overnight, I went from working through the rudimentary stories in *Latin for the New Millennium* to analyzing some of the most sophisticated rhetoric of the ancient world. Latin paradoxically allows for both specificity and broad ambiguity, and the translator determines the exact syntax in the former and takes creative liberties in translating the latter. I was enthralled by the mechanics of Latin, and the ways each writer bent them to his own needs; however, I didn't yet have the confidence to engage with the texts. One day, a classmate neglected to adjust for the case of a noun demanded by a rarely used irregular verb. When, without thinking, I raised my hand to correct him, I realized I finally understood some of the quirks of the language.

From then on, I was confident enough to feel like I was engaging with each ancient author one-on-one. Latin was opening up entirely new (and old) worlds to me. When I read Caesar's *De Bello Gallico,* I pictured myself as a loyal legionary receiving secret military intelligence about the Gallic Wars. Reading Pliny's letters, I began to imagine that he was writing me personal anecdotes about the pleasures of catching boars in the woods or the harrowing eruption of Mount Vesuvius.

The word "translation" comes from the Latin *trans*, "across," and *latum*, "borne or carried," and my favorite moments of translating come from bringing different disciplines together through a close reading of sometimes just a single word. In Vergil's Aeneid, for instance, I came across one of multiple words for "anchor," *ancora*. Curious why Vergil had chosen this particular word, I looked up the historical accounts of ancient Roman technology and discovered that *ancora* was anachronistic: though common in Virgil's own time, this type of anchor could not have existed when the Aeneid takes place. I happily found myself at the intersection of history, science, and Latin.

Writing a lab report for AP Chemistry or solving math problems in BC Calculus is primarily a solitary endeavor, but translating Latin is a collaborative effort. I work alongside my classmates and centuries of classical scholars who have grappled with the same texts and offered insights through appended notes. In Pliny's account of Mount Vesuvius' eruption, a footnote advised us to compare the eruption's effects in Pompeii vs. Herculaneum. My teacher brought in rocks he excavated from Pompeii, showing us Plinian bombs, explaining why they did not appear at Herculaneum, and a classmate drew us a map of the geography between Vesuvius, Pompeii, and Herculaneum; together, we developed a comprehensive picture of the eruption.

In practice, translating is a highly technical task, but the concept is simple: make an unfamiliar language accessible to a new audience. I can apply many skills I have learned from translating Latin to my other interests. When writing science research abstracts, I closely analyze the dense source material before translating it for a lay audience. Conversely, I can translate real-world problems into scientific experiments that aim to provide concrete solutions. When I chant Torah and Haftarah in front of my synagogue's congregation, I convey the meaning of biblical Hebrew words through the ancient melody, or trope, with which each word must be sung. In band, I imbue sheet music with tone and emotion while mindful of my individual role in serving a larger ensemble. As an editor of my school newspaper, I translate news and feature stories to the student body through assigning and revising articles. In all that I do, I translate to make sense of the world I live in and to share my understanding with others.

ESSAY 2 (YALE SUPPLEMENT): PLEASE REFLECT ON SOMETHING YOU WOULD LIKE US TO KNOW ABOUT YOU THAT WE MIGHT NOT LEARN FROM THE REST OF YOUR APPLICATION, OR ON SOMETHING ABOUT WHICH YOU WOULD LIKE TO SAY MORE.

On my first day of Rockefeller University's Summer Science Research Program (SSRP), I knocked on the door of room B322 holding a pair of plastic goggles, but instead of a laboratory full of beakers and test tubes, I found myself in an office full of computers. When a post-doc sat me down at a desktop and told me it would be my workspace for the next two months, I realized that the summer would be very different from my expectations.

The head of the lab informed me my job would be to analyze the genes of patients with Crohn's disease to better understand the pathogenesis of the disease and treatment options. Although it was beyond the scope of the original project, my curiosity led me to question the researchers about important genomic and biostatistical concepts like linkage disequilibrium, p-values, and single nucleotide polymorphisms. To fully answer these questions, I reviewed scientific literature in multiple disciplines: computer science, statistics, genetic sequencing, and Crohn's disease.

With this background, I explored the data sets I was given and proposed an experiment to the head of my lab with the goal of explaining why Eastern European Jews are disproportionately affected by the disease. I did not find novel genes responsible for Crohn's in this population; however, upon further analysis, I discovered that a subset of patients with specific genetic mutations did not respond to a standard treatment. This work has the potential to eventually select optimal therapies based on patients' genetic markers. After two poster presentations on the material, the lab head is in the process of publishing a paper with the results.

Beyond the lab, the SSRP scheduled speakers and activities that allowed me to connect my interests in science, journalism, and humor. Listening to Ivan Oransky, the co-founder of Retraction Watch, I thought about scientific fraud alongside journalistic integrity and discovered that my values as a scientist and journalist overlap. Workshops with Irondale, an improvisational comedy troupe, improved my communication skills by pointing out the scientific jargon I unconsciously used when explaining my research.

Of all of these activities, the most memorable was a visit to the Metropolitan Museum of Art with other members of the program. I had visited the museum on countless occasions, yet moving through the rooms chronologically for the first time provided a visual representation of a narrative bridging art, language, and culture that had been taking place since the beginning of human history. I realized my work had joined a similar narrative, one of science and discovery, and felt inspired and proud of my small contribution.

Rockefeller taught me more about being a scientist than any textbook had; no single experiment existed in a vacuum. Instead, I examined what had been done before and found a new avenue for pushing forward our collective knowledge. My work in the lab taught me that the future narrative of scientific research will integrate multiple disciplines—I cannot wait to be a part of that narrative.

ESSAY 3 (YALE SUPPLEMENT): WHY DOES YALE APPEAL TO YOU?

As an academic omnivore, I would explore courses in multiple fields of interest in Yale's two week shopping period, knowing that whatever classes I chose would be taught by world-class faculty.

At Yale, where scientists are classicists and writers take multivariable calculus, I would feel right at home, especially because home would be the close-knit community of a residential college for all four years.

Outside of classes, I would report on SciTech for the *Yale Daily News* and audition as a clarinetist for the Concert Band or Precision Marching Band. On weekends I would attend services at the Slifka Center and explore New Haven's famous pizzerias. The only challenge would be the long walk from Old Campus to Science Hill; thankfully, I love my bicycle.

ESSAY 4 (YALE SUPPLEMENT): SHORT TAKES

The two qualities I most admire in other people are . . .
determination and compassion

I am most proud of . . .
   my weekly section in *The Record*
I couldn't live without . . .
   The New Yorker, NPR, and green tea
Who or what inspires you?
   Lin-Manuel Miranda and CRISPR
What do you wish you were better at being or doing?
   Seeking out help when I need it
Most Yale freshmen live in suites of four to six students. What would you contribute to the dynamic of your suite?
   study playlists and positive energy

ESSAY 5 (YALE SUPPLEMENT): WHY DO THESE AREAS APPEAL TO YOU? (ECOLOGY & EVOLUTIONARY BIOLOGY, CLASSICS)

Many scientific problems no longer fall neatly into categories of biology, chemistry, physics, or mathematics. By studying molecular biophysics and biochemistry or chemical engineering (specifically biomolecular engineering), I would be collaborating with others to devise unique, interdisciplinary solutions to real-world problems in areas such as treatment for diseases and sustainability while preparing myself for a career in the field.

I also want to study Classics to discover Greco-Roman language, culture, and history and recognize parallels with our modern world. An understanding of the ancient world can provide insights into contemporary life, whether in policy-making, interpersonal relations, or the narrative of scientific discoveries. At Yale, I could read Ovid's *Metamorphoses* or learn about Roman food and drink (but hopefully not have to eat any of it!)

Bryce Crawford

Hometown: San Antonio, TX
Year: Sophomore
College: Benjamin Franklin
Major(s): Mathematics; Physics
Extracurriculars: Navy ROTC; Chaplain's
Office

PROFILE

The summer before his senior year, Bryce Crawford filed into a classroom at the U.S. Naval Academy—complete with a model nuclear reactor—for a course on nuclear engineering. He had traveled a long way from his home in San Antonio, Texas, to attend the weeklong summer camp, and he listened attentively as the course instructor recalled the days he had spent as a navy submarine officer.

These stories piqued Bryce's interest almost as much as the class itself. Back in Texas after the program was over, he began watching YouTube documentaries about submarines, and the more he learned, the more he felt his fascination deepen. "I see a submarine as a kind of spaceship underwater," he explains. "The bottom of the ocean is a place we know very little about, and there's a lot of military value to investing in submarines."

When the time came to apply for college, Bryce, who was the leader of his high school's Army Junior Reserve Officers' Training Corps, knew he wanted a college with a highly ranked physics department and an on-campus ROTC program. Now a member of Yale's class of 2020, Bryce is double majoring in math and physics. He's part of the inaugural group of students in Benjamin Franklin College who moved into the brand-new facility in the fall of 2017.

Most mornings, Bryce wakes up a few hours before his fellow classmates for Navy ROTC programming, which is usually a lecture course or physical training. But the time he spends with his fellow midshipmen is not overbearing for Bryce, who also spends time working at the Chaplain's Office on Old Campus. As a first-year student, he was a regular visitor to the office, taking advantage of the free ice cream for students in between classes. He now works in the Breathing Space, an electronics-free zone affiliated with the Chaplain's Office, and the Buddhist Shrine, a place where students can go to meditate on campus. In addition, Bryce walks the university chaplain's springer spaniel, Phil, and helps run Global Grounds, a relaxed space for students to unwind in the evening on weekends.

Bryce also makes a point of exploring New Haven. He keeps a spreadsheet with all the restaurants he's visited around New Haven and in neighboring towns and says that so far, he's eaten at more than sixty-five different establishments. He says he tries to eat at a new place every Saturday night. Still, his best moments at Yale have been on-campus, he admits—especially nights spent watching movies with friends on the lawn chairs he keeps in his dorm room.

After graduating from Yale, Bryce will devote a minimum of five years to the navy in return for tuition. The work may be highly technical, but it also opens doors, he says. For instance, through ROTC, he's been able to travel to India for a summer language program in the Himalayas.

"If you're willing to spend six months a year under water,

there's a lot of benefits," Bryce says. "It's one of the coolest military jobs there is."

Bryce's essays include one of his Yale supplemental essays.

ESSAY 1 (YALE SUPPLEMENT): PLEASE REFLECT ON SOMETHING YOU WOULD LIKE US TO KNOW ABOUT YOU THAT WE MIGHT NOT LEARN FROM THE REST OF YOUR APPLICATION, OR ON SOMETHING ABOUT WHICH YOU WOULD LIKE TO SAY MORE.

I grew up loving superheroes. Individuals that take it upon themselves to risk their lives to help their society are definitely worth admiration. For instance, Bruce Wayne is exceptionally physically fit, a successful businessman, and has the mind of the most brilliant detective. Tony Stark is an extremely gifted engineer and entrepreneur. Peter Parker is a resourceful scientist, artist (photography is art), and family man. These are ideals I have wanted to live up to since I first watched Saturday morning cartoons. We can't ever be exactly like them, but I want to convince the people around me that we can all be superheroes in small ways. Things as simple as a kind greeting and a helping hand can make someone else's life a lot better.

College is like a second coming of age with a *Lord of the Flies* twist. The college community I want to be a part of is a group of friends that raise one another when our parents are no longer here to do it. Setting examples for one another and being heroes in each other's lives is exactly what we'll need if we want this to be a positive and enriching experience. I plan on being a helping hand to the people around me. In high school I've done that by tutoring my friends for free and participating in community service. In college I see no reason why that wouldn't continue. My perspective is that of a community leader, one who wants people to work together to help one another past our individual shortcomings.

My chemistry teacher has been one of my favorite teachers because he never fails to teach beyond the required curriculum, including oftentimes giving us life advice. His number one item on a list of things we need to find while in college was a support group. This group would be a small group of close friends that we could count on for anything. I want the people in the environment around me to know that they can count on me when the going gets tough—that's the person I want to be remembered as.

Hana Davis

Hometown: Hong Kong

Year: Sophomore

College: Morse

Major(s): Architecture

Extracurriculars: *Yale Daily News*, Weekend
section editor; Hong Kong Students
Association, president

PROFILE

Growing up in Hong Kong, Hana Davis wore the same over-sized Yale sweater to sleep every night—the sweater her father had bought thirty years ago as a law student at Yale. She knew she wanted to be a Yalie since she was a child, in part because of her *Gossip Girl* obsession at age thirteen (the show's main character, Blair Waldorf, had a similar infatuation with the school of Yale's bulldog mascot, Handsome Dan). As a high school senior, Hana had her heart set on Yale, though she encourages others to keep an open mind and consider a variety of colleges during the college admissions process.

Today, that worn-out sweater, a reminder of home, hangs in Hana's dorm room closet in Morse College. A sophomore architecture major, she splits her free time between writing and illustrating for the *Yale Layer* (an undergraduate magazine focused on mental health), editing the *Yale Daily News* Weekend section, and leading the Hong Kong

Students Association. In light of her activist parents and upbringing in Hong Kong, it's no surprise that Hana has fostered a fighting spirit and passion for human rights, with regards to Hong Kong's autonomy from China in particular. Outside of her classes and extracurriculars, Hana is also a student in the Multidisciplinary Academic Program in Human Rights, an undergraduate program offered by Yale Law School.

In high school, Hana spent most of her time on the field, on the court, or in a studio by way of various sports teams and dance classes (she admits that she is now far less physically active at Yale, where she has shifted her extracurricular focus toward writing). She was never one for debate competitions or Model United Nations conferences. Rather, Hana preferred to paint, sculpt, or photograph. She says that she has always had a passion for art, her favorite International Baccalaureate subject from high school.

When Hana arrived at Yale, she had no intention of ever pursuing art in the classroom. Her parents suggested she consider architecture, but Hana—who identified as a prospective history, political science, or Ethnicity, Race, & Migration major—laughed at the idea. But she was willing to give Introduction to Architecture a chance.

It was there, sitting for a lecture in Linsly-Chittenden Hall, that Hana realized her parents might have had a point. As the professor presented the architectural dilemma faced by city planners considering what might arise after the Berlin Wall had been torn down, Hana understood that the field was the perfect combination of all of her interests.

"Coming here has only proved—maybe me kind of being overly obsessed with Yale wasn't misplaced," Hana chuckled.

Hana's essays include her Common App personal statement and one of her Yale supplemental essays.

ESSAY 1 (COMMON APP):
PERSONAL STATEMENT

Some students have a background, identity, interest, or talent that is so meaningful they believe their application would be incomplete without it. If this sounds like you, then please share your story.

I was raised in the streets.

I grew up sitting on my father's shoulders, my tiny head sticking out above a mass of thousands. I grew up marching between my parents in an orderly line, down crowded Hong Kong streets. I grew up sitting on the ground of Victoria Park, every year on the anniversary of the Tiananmen massacre, with a brightly glowing candle cupped between my ever-growing hands.

When I was a baby, I would lie in my crib with my tiny hands curled into tight fists, one arm raised above my head as if punching the air in indignation. My mother would laugh and say I was born a fighter. There's a photo of me from around the age of five, where I'm standing on a crowded Hong Kong street. I doubt I had any clue at the time as to why I was there, but the sense of determination and infectious fervor were clearly reflected in my eyes.

That same perseverance and spirit were reflected again in my eyes, and in the eyes of thousands of other Hong Kong students during the Umbrella Movement. As I sat on the highway with the thick humid air hanging over the city, I felt a cool calm because I sensed in that moment a feeling of empowerment—not because I knew China would back down, or that our efforts would succeed, but because I felt that in that moment I had millions of people supporting me, working with me and helping me. It was the first time I had truly understood the power of the masses.

That day, as I cautiously made my way to Central, an indescribable feeling surged in my chest as I neared the crowds. I sat on the freeway in a lopsided circle with my friends, instead of within the protective shield of my parents as I had done countless times before. We snacked and joked and studied for upcoming exams, yet we could all feel, in the lighthearted atmosphere, a sense of unexpressed tension, a feeling of dignified resistance.

That was the first time I had gone alone to a protest. That was the first time I had truly been present in a movement. That was the first time I was utterly aware of what was going on; the first time I had felt an absolute resolve to do my best to fight for my beliefs and defend our rights. That was the day before unthinkable violence broke out on the streets of my hometown.

We had a discussion once in Chinese class about the Occupy Central movement. Virtually all in my class were against the movement for a variety of reasons, mainly the inconvenience it caused them; everyone, that is, except me. I stood in defense of the revolution, in defense of Hong Kong's need for democracy, in defense of the thousands of people sitting out on the streets for months, being braver than I could possibly imagine.

With a human rights lawyer for a father and a political scientist for a mother, I've never known another reality.

ESSAY 2 (YALE SUPPLEMENT): PLEASE REFLECT ON SOMETHING YOU WOULD LIKE US TO KNOW ABOUT YOU THAT WE MIGHT NOT LEARN FROM THE REST OF YOUR APPLICATION, OR ON SOMETHING ABOUT WHICH YOU WOULD LIKE TO SAY MORE.

> "Art, freedom and creativity will change society faster than politics."
>
> —*Victor Pinchuk*

The dying sun filters through the forest of buildings and illuminates the dust in the air, saturating the messy room with a golden tinge and creating an ephemeral beauty reminiscent of Satis House.

The symphony of screeching tires, hocking hawkers, and

bargaining shoppers filter through open windows. The smell of freshly squeezed paint combines with the waft of stinky tofu and grilled charsiu from the street below; the sensory explosion is complete.

As the music in my ear swells to a crescendo my brush touches the canvas. The clouds in my mind clear up and my vision tunnels onto my painting. I morph into something unearthly. The brush becomes an extension of my arm; the canvas a protective shell; and the paint, like oxygen pulsing through my veins, becomes an integral part of my survival.

I've become one with 'my' corner of the brightly colored, albeit cramped and messy studio. Like my bones, the four walls are part of the architecture of my being.

Painting has always been a pleasure I hold dear to my heart. It's the weight that grounds me when I'm about to float off. However, for me, art is not simply an enjoyable pastime.

Art informs my world—from my passion for human rights, to my voracious appetite for global news, to my penchant for pleasure reading, and my adoration of words—art is the net that binds my interests and the lens that colours my perspective.

I don't view my passions in isolation; I believe they're all irretrievably linked within me. Art has tinted my outlook on the world and taught me to view situations from a different angle. It has given me creativity and an appreciation of how easily societies can be swayed. From Ai Weiwei's provocative art to Mao's propaganda posters, art contributes to political struggles, speaks to fear, and reaches masses in a way that no other media can. Art transcends time and space; it breaks language barriers and touches and unites the world in an utterly unique way.

In literature, I am pulled by an unseen magnetic field toward sentences and words that are beautiful in appearance and sound. Just as certain art has the ability to stun me into silence, I have always been spellbound by the magic a few letters can hold. To me, novels are mystical combinations of word and letter creating powerful spells. As Leonardo da Vinci eloquently expressed, "Painting is poetry that is seen rather than felt, and poetry is painting that is felt rather than seen."

My passions are woven together by the yarn of art into a tapestry of creativity and a desire to help the world. With the firmest of convictions, I believe Henry Van Dyke's words: "Use the talents you possess, the woods would be very silent if no birds sang there except those that sang best;" and with my paint-splattered hands, that is precisely what I endeavour to do.

Drew Gupta

Hometown: Charleston, WV

Year: Sophomore

College: Branford

Major(s): Molecular, Cellular, & Developmental Biology (MCDB)

Extracurriculars: *Yale Journal of Human Rights*, founder; Yale Global Medical Brigades, president

PROFILE

For most high school students, their daily worries include school, family, friends and extracurriculars. But, in 2014, Drew Gupta's hometown—Charleston, West Virginia—suffered one of the largest chemical contaminations in U.S. history.

As thousands of gallons of the industrial chemical MCHM spilled into a local water supply, many residents of Drew's hometown were unable to drink the water for weeks. Children were especially affected, and Drew was given the entire month of January off from school.

The catastrophe inspired Drew to begin thinking about the world, and its problems, in a more serious and deliberate way. Drew has since spent his career as a student focusing on health policy and medicine. At Yale, he hopes to take advantage of the University's five-year BA–BS/Master of Public Health program and is currently a neurobiology major on the premedical track.

"Something happened with the water crisis that made me

realize, Wow, Yale is absolutely the best place for this," Drew says.

Drew's favorite part of Yale is its diversity of classes. While some Yale classes survey huge fields of study, he says, others go into depth on a single topic. Comparing his time at Yale to high school, he notes that the academics are "surprisingly easier" in New Haven—not because the subject matter is easier, but because he is able to take classes of genuine interest to him that do not feel boring.

But Drew's Yale experience has not been all about classes or medicine. For him, college is primarily an opportunity to "broaden" his mind and, in his case, explore everything Yale's New Haven campus has to offer.

With an abundance of extracurriculars to choose from, Drew has not shied away from getting deeply involved in various activities. From cofounding the *Yale Journal of Human Rights* to serving as president of Yale Global Medical Brigades, he finds time to balance his commitments and still hang out with his friends, including his twin brother and fellow Yale student, Arka Gupta.

"All your friends are within max a 10 to 15 minute walk away from you. To have so many peers around you . . . is just very valuable," he said.

In fact, one of Drew's fondest memories is the annual Yale–Harvard football game. There, he said, you get to hang out with all your closest friends and unite against "one common enemy" for a weekend full of concerts and late-night dancing.

Still, Drew says that playing the balancing game between his different engagements is not an easy task. And it is important, he adds, to also find time to relax with some time alone.

Drew's essays include his Common App personal statement and two Yale supplemental essays.

ESSAY 1 (COMMON APP):
PERSONAL STATEMENT

CALL ME BILLY

Pressed against my jugular artery as I was about to drown in a puddle of my own blood, a four-inch blade was my first introduction to health disparities in Appalachia.

Earlier that morning, I had enjoyed waking up in the semi-dilapidated "hollar" of my host family to the melodious chirping of birds, the scampering of squirrels, and the shouts of laughter as kids played. Even though the cold tap water had been poisoned from forty years of coal mining, a warm feeling of acceptance emanated in Welch, West Virginia. As the day advanced, so did the thermostat, and an enormous crowd of homeless individuals gathered to escape midmorning starvation and the blazing sun. Once a center of economic prosperity, the area now embodied despair, poverty and addiction.

Volunteering to distribute donated food supplies to church-going residents on a Sunday morning, I wasn't expecting much action. Nevertheless, a hunched-back man in his fifties wearing scruffy denim overalls had to make things a little interesting. He passed me a box of tomatoes to hand out. Being courteous, I responded "Thank you sir"—that's all I had said. Unfortunately, he took it the wrong way; he preferred that I call him by his real name: Billy. My new acquaintance "Billy" then unsheathed his Swiss-army knife, tracing it against my neck.

At that moment, I feared for my life. Was I supposed to defend myself in this melee match of death, or surrender and cry for help? My jugular was one sloppy jerk away from flooding the floor with my own blood. My eyes darted toward my identical twin across the kitchen and I felt afraid not just for my life, but also his. After what seemed like hours, the man muttered, "Don't call me sir. Call me Billy." Moving beyond our little misunderstanding, we got to know more about each other. I told Billy some interesting tidbits about myself, like how I binge-watch Bollywood movies (at least the ones available on Netflix) or my obsession in constantly checking my Twitter feed. In contrast to my lighthearted habits, Billy revealed to me the events that have shaped his life story. Billy was raised in a humble shack with no electricity or running water and abused by a single alcoholic mother living in a county with a life expectancy at par with Haiti. He wished he could have earned his high school diploma, but had to drop out to support his mom and younger brothers by working in West Virginia's coal mines. Billy's situation exemplified a lack of opportunity that profoundly contradicted my prior philosophy that anyone, no matter what their circumstances, could pursue their aspirations as they saw fit. Billy felt powerless to either advance his socio-economic class or escape from the clench of poverty. While I was taught the concept of personal ambition and individualism as a way to control one's destiny, Billy could afford to focus on only one goal—survival.

When one suffers a lifetime of poverty, it manifests itself in the greatest inequality of all: healthcare. Billy and many others in a similar situation face disproportionate rates of obesity, diabetes, cardiovascular disease, premature teen pregnancy, substance abuse (especially opioid addiction), mental illness, suicide and the list goes on. Because of the economic situation, these folks are forced to prioritize saving a few bucks instead of their own well-being. If we as a society hope to help those who need it most, we must build a solid infrastructure for supporting social determinants of health. As an aspiring physician, I understand that healthcare is not limited to just four walls of a clinic, but to entire communities. Prescribing a pill isn't enough in the 21st century to treat a disease; instead, we need to provide a stable job market, suitable living environment and opportunity. If the aforementioned are accomplished, then we can help my friend Billy back in Welch, WV.

ESSAY 2 (YALE SUPPLEMENT): PLEASE REFLECT ON SOMETHING YOU WOULD LIKE US TO KNOW ABOUT YOU THAT WE MIGHT NOT LEARN FROM THE REST OF YOUR APPLICATION, OR ON SOMETHING ABOUT WHICH YOU WOULD LIKE TO SAY MORE.

Every U.S. citizen deserves the human right to access clean water—but that was violated in my hometown. In January of 2014, 4-methylcyclohexanemethanol (to make it easier, let's abbreviate to MCHM) leaked into the Elk River and contaminated the water supply for 300,000 West Virginia residents. For weeks, one could not drink, shower, cook, clean nor wash with the water without risking the chance of nausea, vomiting, dizziness, diarrhea, reddened skin, rashes and even cancer. Despite assurances from state officials that the water was safe, everyone was skeptical because the black-licorice odor still lingered. As a trained interviewer in a community-based research initiative, I assisted in evaluating the impact of this unprecedented historical event on residents' physical, mental and economic health. This study revealed a negative psychological impact, making me wonder: What happened inside our brains that causes us so much stress?

While working on an AP Psychology assignment on neuroanatomy (a fancy term for parts of the brain), a revelation suddenly dawned upon me. Of all human senses, only smell is not routed through the sensory processing center known as the thalamus. So while smell warns us about the water, taste says otherwise and encourages us to drink to be hydrated. This psycho-physiological melee between olfaction (smell) and gustation (taste) is essentially two independent entities combating one another for dominance, the anatomical dilemma that leads to anxiety and depression.

Discovering this phenomenon, I immediately published my research in the state's largest newspaper to educate others. I was startled to receive a call from a faculty at the Johns Hopkins Bloomberg School of Public Health (Dr. Henry Taylor) requesting my permission to utilize this hypothesis as a case study for graduate students. What started as an AP Psych assignment mixed with a dash of inquisitiveness evolved into a theory that was crucial to our state's recovery from this federally declared disaster.

I was truly thrilled by the opportunity to contribute to the academic conversation surrounding response and resiliency, but my mind once again wondered, "Are we any better prepared for another disaster?" I wanted to do more to create an injury prevention atmosphere and so began studying the concepts of emergency preparedness in youth. With paucity of existing evidence, I realized that to engage my fellow students, I must speak their language: YouTube! So, I traveled across the world (Lake Zurich, Taj Mahal, and even Pittsburgh) to film a video on risk communication and youth preparedness encompassing cultural, language and other barriers often uncovered during emergencies. After winning a national video competition, I was invited to complete an internship at the Harvard T. H. Chan School of Public Health. Working with scientists on innovative and trendsetting research in youth emergency risk communication, I recently submitted my project to the Centers for Disease Control and Prevention (CDC). While I was thrust into the field due to a disaster, I now look forward to the opportunity to continue my research endeavors and further strengthen my fundamentals in public health science.

ESSAY 3 (YALE SUPPLEMENT):
WHY DOES YALE APPEAL TO YOU?

Chatting with a Yale Student Ambassador inspired me to explore all the university has to offer.

After diligent research, I discovered a gem that only Yale offers: a five-year B.A.–B.S./M.P.H. degree program. Incorporating my previous experiences of promoting health awareness in McDowell County and an internship with the Harvard TH Chan School of Public Health, I hope to continue my endeavors in this interdisciplinary field.

Alex Hoganson

Hometown: Washington, DC

Year: Sophomore

College: Branford

Major(s): Mechanical Engineering

Extracurriculars: Yale Undergraduate Aerospace Association; Branford College Council

PROFILE

Alex Hoganson calculates that he probably spends more hours in the Yale Center for Engineering Innovation and Design (CEID) than in his own room. "I enjoy designing and creating things," he says, shrugging good-naturedly.

Perhaps unsurprisingly, Alex, who now majors in mechanical engineering, was passionate about the sciences long before he enrolled at Yale. He attended Thomas Jefferson High School for Science and Technology, a renowned magnet school near Washington, D.C., that focuses on STEM. Alex says he's especially grateful to his high school for the opportunity to meet people with whom he shared interests.

Prior to coming to college, Alex was heavily involved with volunteering and community service, racking up hundreds of hours and more than a decade of hard work. Unfortunately, Alex hasn't been able to find as much time for community service as he had hoped he would at Yale.

When he's not designing rockets in the CEID or keeping up with his heavy course load, Alex pens the occasional humor piece for the *Yale Record* and frequents the Branford College Council. He also participates in Süperfly, Yale's men's Ultimate Frisbee team, and is heavily involved in the Yale Undergraduate Aerospace Association, which is especially relevant since he intends to pursue a career in the field. He says he dreams of designing the next generation of Mars rovers.

As a STEM major at a liberal arts school, Alex does sometimes feel as though his life and interests diverge from his peers', both academically and socially. He classifies himself as "the type of guy [who] would much rather play board games than go out to a frat," and his fondest weekend memories have generally involved staying in to continue interesting conversations with his friends and peers. He also frequently visits the Branford Tea Room, which provides a cozy, relaxed environment and is always stocked with hot beverages and snacks.

Alex's essays include his Common App personal statement.

ESSAY 1 (COMMON APP):
PERSONAL STATEMENT
Some students have a background, identity, interest, or talent that is so meaningful they believe their application would be incomplete without it.

"So what's your excuse for skipping practice this time, *slacker?*"

I cringed away from the belligerent voice of my track captain.

"I—I have a meeting. We're deciding what activities to have for this year's Global Youth Service day, and—"

He loudly cut me off:

"You know none of this service stuff matters, right? You're not REALLY helping anybody. All you're doing is padding your college resume and ditching practice!"

I tried to explain to him that I helped people, and that I honestly enjoyed volunteering and actually cared about what I did, but my opinions went in one ear and out the other. Conversely, *his* words settled in my mind and left a seed of doubt. Were all the years and the many hours I had spent volunteering making a meaningful difference?

The earliest time I can remember doing community service is third grade. My family and I went to play Bingo at a senior living center. I was terrified of being surrounded by scary strangers, but their faces lit up when I sat near them. I connected with the elderly residents and made them laugh and smile.

With my enthusiastic support, our family set a goal of accomplishing one hundred acts of community service. For years, I sacrificed soccer, weekends, and holidays to volunteer. I visited homeless shelters, Alzheimer's patients, and food pantries. As I got older, I started doing more on my own, or with other teens. There have been some rough days; people slamming doors in my face and ripping up leaflets in front of me. However, volunteering in my community always has helped me to feel grounded and connected with others. Undoubtedly, I've come a long way since my first Bingo game, yet the emotional high I experience from interacting with people is still fresh and invigorating. Now, I am trying to volunteer on a whole new level by learning how to teach teens to start their own volunteer projects and to get them funded. Unfortunately, since that day at practice, Chris's taunts have sometimes run around in my head. Am I making a real difference?

Recently, a brief conversation silenced those occasional doubts. Since freshman year, I have volunteered with my school's Black Student Union's TJ Inspire program, which seeks to inspire a passion for STEM in local, lower-income minority elementary students. I enjoyed spending my Saturdays engaging students in exciting, hands-on science experiments.

Last month, I was entreating incoming freshmen to sign up to volunteer with our program when a girl with a striking Afro boldly walked up to me. When I started to introduce myself to the freshmen, she cut me off.

"I know who you are!" she said, looking up at me excitedly. "I remember you!"

She then described how at a TJ inspire session, I had helped her to understand a potato-clock lab and encouraged her to pursue her interest in science by applying to my STEM-focused high school. As I continued talking with her, I had a hard time concealing my excitement. I had inspired someone to follow her passion, and helped her to change her life.

Captain Chris always used to say that nothing beats a runner's high. For me, volunteering comes close. He's gone now, away at college. I doubt he'd even remember our brief conversation—or care that he was wrong. But more important than proving a point to an old antagonist is my realization that while the rewards for my efforts might not be immediately obvious, they exist nonetheless. My passion for volunteering that began years ago has become a habit that, like running, I will continue throughout my life. I love helping others, and my volunteering represents an intrinsic part of who I am. My family still hasn't performed 100 volunteer acts, but I look forward to celebrating each event.

Jackson Lindley

Hometown: Rancho Mirage, CA

Year: Sophomore

College: Davenport

Major(s): Political Science

Extracurriculars: Air Force ROTC; Chi Psi Fraternity

PROFILE

Jackson Lindley credits the Air Force Reserve Officer Training Corps for giving him his best friendships and his favorite memories at Yale. A cadet in the university's detachment, he says that taking his oath of enlistment during the first week of his first year felt like "stepping into the next chapter of [his] life."

It is a chapter he had planned for years. Jackson says he always knew that he wanted to be in the military, even as a boy growing up in Rancho Mirage, California. Being part of the Civil Air Patrol in California allowed him to train with officers and develop his "outdoorsy" side through backpacking, hiking, and even conducting search and recovery patrols.

As a high school senior, Jackson applied to Yale, the U.S. Naval Academy and the U.S. Air Force Academy. He says he ultimately decided to attend Yale because of its diverse student body and cooperative community.

"I'm so fortunate to be exposed to the people here," Jackson says. "They're the ones who set it apart and set it above. I've been able to grow more through talking with friends than being in class."

But it's been a long road to success, he adds. Being in New Haven has been a process of making mistakes and getting into a groove, something he describes as "growing into Yale." Now, though, he can't imagine being anywhere else.

When he's not hanging out with his fellow Davenport suitemates, Jackson is active in Greek life on campus through the Chi Psi fraternity. He is also certified as an emergency medical technician. Even though he never joined an a cappella group at Yale, citing how its unpredictable time schedule could potentially conflict with his ROTC obligations, he says he has sung with jazz combos and orchestras and loved it.

Jackson adds that he "coasted" through high school and got a crash course in focus and time management once he came to Yale. Outside of what he has learned as a political science major, he has figured out how to work within the school's institutional constraints and "get Yale to work for [his] own opportunities."

But he says Yale's most valuable lessons have been on how to listen, communicate, and understand the opinions of others.

"I count myself lucky to be able to talk to people with such diverse opinions," Jackson says. "In the Air Force, you're going to be interacting with people from all different kinds of cultures . . . I try to take [Yale's diversity] in and allow it to influence me so I can apply it in the future."

Jackson's essays include his Common App personal statement and one of his Yale supplemental essays.

ESSAY 1 (COMMON APP):
PERSONAL STATEMENT

It hit with the sound of an explosion. A wave of gravel and sand stung my face and I had to lean into the force to stay upright. One moment I was standing in the protected calm of a 24-by-20 military command tent; then in an instant I was outside, and the world went brown. It was a gale force blast of wind that tore the 400-pound metal and canvas structure from its stakes and tossed it in the air like a plastic bag. I heard screams and saw several of my cadets go down. The heavy tent had plowed forward before it went up. Now their eyes were on me. This weekend had just changed in a very serious way.

It was a three-day Civil Air Patrol mission in Indio, California. I was the cadet Project Officer in charge of twenty cadets providing support and security for the Desert Triathlon. One might wonder why a sixteen-year-old student was in that position. The answer starts back a long time in my relatively brief existence. I have wanted to serve as an officer in the US Military as far back as I can remember. I have an "All about me" drawing from second grade when I listed my future occupation as "working on an aircraft carrier" followed by being the President. I was an ambitious seven-year-old. When I was eight I attended a football game at the Air Force Academy. At the tailgate party before the game I was introduced to "Ben, he flies F-22's" and "This is Niles. He's a Special Operator and can't tell us what he does." They were in shorts and t-shirts, flipping hamburgers, and talking to me about the most amazing things I could imagine. I wanted to be them. It has not changed.

I was already involved in Scouting. I learned the basics of survival, first aid, and leadership, earning the rank of Eagle when I was twelve. I loved it. Then I discovered Civil Air Patrol, a civilian auxiliary of the Air Force. I went all in. The training and responsibility went to a higher level. I was learning the importance of supporting my leaders, who were teaching me how to lead by example.

We had been battling the wind for two days, which was much worse for the 1,000 athletes competing. In all, there were about 3,000 people there. Coordinating the parking and securing the competition bikes was our job. Organizing the team, and keeping them safe, was my responsibility. Now I was doing concussion testing. We determined three cadets needed to be taken to an urgent care. I was walking to the vehicle with one of the cadets, who was protesting that she was fine, when she slumped against me. I caught her and carried her to the truck. I looked at the senior member nearby and said, "She needs attention now." He pulled out his phone and dialed 911. When they left in the ambulances I focused on the remaining team and the mission. It poured rain all the next day, and at the end the Race Director told me it was the toughest event in his twenty-five years of competition, and he couldn't have done it without our team. Battered, bruised, cold, and wet, I was so proud of every cadet. I had been awake for 40 hours, the three injured cadets were going to be fine, and I felt great.

I once listened to an Air Force General explain that basically there are our homes, and there are our enemies, with a dangerous space in between. Most of my life has been spent preparing me to stand and lead in that space. I am looking forward to a university experience where I can learn, contribute, and mature as a leader. Whatever comes my way in the next thirty days and the next thirty years, I want to be the one who is always ready when the big storms come.

ESSAY 2 (YALE SUPPLEMENTAL): PLEASE REFLECT ON SOMETHING YOU WOULD LIKE US TO KNOW ABOUT YOU THAT WE MIGHT NOT LEARN FROM THE REST OF YOUR APPLICATION, OR ON SOMETHING ABOUT WHICH YOU WOULD LIKE TO SAY MORE.

I sing. It is not just something I do, it is part of who I am. I have grown up around music. My mother sings opera and I am told that when I was two she heard me humming a cartoon theme. She grabbed my dad and said, "He's on key!"

Humming sounds turned into singing words, and I have never gotten tired of it. I can't say I loved it from the beginning, or even knew the meaning of it. My mom had to pay me ten dollars to sing my first duet with her in church. It was after a sixth grade school performance that I realized how much I loved the experience. The applause was great, but I realized how much they loved it too. I saw that music was something the performer and audience enjoyed together.

I began to learn instruments to accompany my vocals. I performed jazz, rock, R&B, country, and even classical. The special moments continued until it wasn't about the moment. It was the story of me.

Most people find it interesting that I sing, especially those who know that my career goal is to be an officer in the United States military. While I don't plan on a career in music, I do plan on a life of music. I took my senior year of science in summer school to open a spot for AP Music Theory, which is taught by my AP Calculus teacher. Math and music have always seemed more alike than different to me. Although I intend to study engineering in college, I also intend to sing. Whenever I hear about Yale, the music is always mentioned. The ability to be part of three hundred years of history would be an incredible honor.

An important chapter came at the end of my sophomore year. I was asked to sing a solo with a full orchestra in our largest local theater. That performance was the first time that I practiced not only singing well, but working with my fifty-four new musical friends to move the emotions of a large audience. The rehearsals were chaotic and intense.

The night of the performance, I was ready. It was a tradition at that theater to sign the wall backstage. I scanned the names looking for an open spot. Johnny Cash, George Burns, Tommy Tune, Bette Midler, and so many other amazing people were there. I humbly selected a spot between Bob Hope and Lucille Ball.

My song was in the second act, and I wasn't nervous, but I had to contain a lot of energy for a really long time. "Jackson, you're next," finally came from the stage manager. My heart was racing as I ran through the opening notes in my head. My cues with the orchestra, my marks on the stage, my personal journey with music were all there. She handed me a mic, said "Break a leg," and gave me push. I stepped out into the light.

Serena Ly

Hometown: Santa Ana, CA

Year: Sophomore

College: Branford

Major(s): Molecular, Cellular & Developmental Biology

Extracurriculars: Dwight Hall at Yale, student executive committee co-coordinator; community health educator; Yale EMS; Yale School of Public Health, research assistant; Alliance for Southeast Asian Students at Yale

PROFILE

During her childhood, Serena Ly would hear stories from her father about living under the Khmer Rouge in Cambodia.

When she embarked on an International Baccalaureate research essay in her senior year of high school, Serena "immediately" chose the Khmer Rouge as her research topic to learn more about her Cambodian roots—and the violence that had affected her family so deeply.

"How could I not write a piece about a time in history that killed millions, devastated a peaceful country, and continues to affect my family and many others to this day?" Serena asks.

She threw herself into her research, methodically gathering books and setting up interviews with family members. Still, despite her preparation, Serena said she had "no idea" how emotional an interview with her father would be.

It was Serena's desire to better understand her intense

response to the difficult past of her father that ultimately inspired her Yale supplementary essay.

"I felt [my father's] pain, the horror he felt, the slow cracking of his spirit," she recalled. "I knew that I had to synthesize some sort of piece where I could attempt to delineate these emotions and the way this interview brought me closer to both him and my Cambodian roots."

Reflecting on her life since applying to Yale, Serena says that she has gained a deeper understanding about contemporary issues facing Cambodia—many of which represent leftover legacies of the Khmer Rouge. She says she now feels an even greater "duty to help" her country.

Serena, a Molecular, Cellular, & Developmental Biology major, takes helping others within her community seriously, whether it be in New Haven or Southeast Asia. As co-coordinator of Dwight Hall, Yale's student-run umbrella service organization, Serena plans and implements service projects at Yale and throughout New Haven, working with Dwight Hall's member groups to ensure that they have the resources necessary to carry out their missions.

"I feel that I have found the most happiness and growth in my experiences off campus as an involved New Haven resident," Serena said. "There are lessons that are simply impossible to learn on campus that can be taught in the city if you just take the chance to immerse yourself as a New Haven resident."

At Yale, Serena is also a community health educator, a member of Yale Emergency Medical Services, a Yale School of Public Health research assistant and a member of the Alliance for Southeast Asian Students at Yale, or ALSEAS.

As a member of ALSEAS, Serena hopes to strengthen Yale's Southeast Asian student community and encourage outreach from the Yale Admissions Office to Southeast Asian students in the United States and internationally. According to Serena,

Yale College has not enrolled a Cambodian international student in decades.

"I hope that changes," Serena said. "I also hope that soon, more and more Cambodian-Americans like me will be given opportunities to attend universities like Yale and to bring the spirit of Cambodian resilience forward and into the public eye."

Serena's essays include her Common App personal statement.

ESSAY 1 (COMMON APP):
PERSONAL STATEMENT

I LISTENED
Equipped with a notepad and blue ink pen, I began my interview with my father, a former refugee and survivor of the Cambodian Killing Fields, to supplement my research project. Inexplicably nervous as I shifted in my seat, I gripped my notepad and locked my eyes on the first question.

"To begin the conversation, prior to the communists' takeover of Cambodia, how would you describe your family life?"

My father replied in a formal tone, clearly struggling to mold his story into the frame I had imposed on him. I had heard stories about the time he broke his leg at his refugee camp and my journalist uncle who disappeared during the regime, but I never fully listened to his attempts to illustrate the past.

I knew about the atrocities of the Khmer Rouge but failed to completely understand its repercussions. The gap between two generations with vastly different experiences always clung to my conscience, exacerbated by the fact that I cannot speak Khmer fluently. I hesitated to speak, fearing judgment for my American accent and imperfect grammar, and desperately desired to liberate myself from this stigma.

As soon as I was assigned the International Baccalaureate Extended Essay to fulfill my diploma requirements, I immediately scribbled in my topic—the economic, political, and social repercussions of the Khmer Rouge's reign in Cambodia—on my proposal sheet and slapped it onto my advisor's desk.

During the interview, I quickly realized the impotency of my questions, which could not capture what I had failed to face my father with: empathy. I slid my notepad aside. In his thick accent, which had traversed thousands of miles and transcended more than thirty years of adversity, he allowed his words to fall limply, as pieces of his story cascaded into pools of raw emotion.

One hour glided by, as he divulged the time he was beaten by a Khmer Rouge soldier. His voice broke.

"It was . . . It was hard."

These laconic words rendered me speechless. I envisioned the prison my father was kept in and the bullets that whizzed past him from a mile away. I felt the agony that surged in him as he watched his mother wither away from starvation.

I had observed Esperanza's coming-of-age as a young Latina woman in *The House on Mango Street*. I had explored Bigger Thomas's tragic bildungsroman in *Native Son*, and in one hour and thirty-eight minutes, I had experienced the most devastating period in Cambodian history from the eyes of one of its lost children.

"*Orkun chraun,* Pa."

Thank you. I may mispronounce a phrase in Khmer. I will definitely misspell every other Khmer word I throw myself at. However, as I have gradually grasped the language, I remember that singular moment of tenderness that introduced me to a sentiment that remains universal. A pen and paper cannot capture the tears we shed for those we have lost, but words can allay the tempestuous memories time has helped us accept and convey to others.

Jacob Malinowski

Hometown: Greendale, WI

Year: Sophomore

College: Grace Hopper

Major(s): Political Science

Extracurriculars: Tour Guide; Students for a New American Politics (SNAP) PAC, chief of staff; Yale International Relations Association

PROFILE

Applying to Yale University was Jacob Malinowski's attempt to thwart destiny.

Most people from his small town of Greendale, Wisconsin, never stray far from home—and, Jacob says, most are destined to return to his town soon after finishing college to start families of their own. But Jacob wanted to take a risk and venture outside of the "homogeneous" Greendale bubble.

As a first-generation college student, Jacob "flew by the seat of [his] pants" during the college admissions process. He looked at smaller liberal arts schools with strong social science programs, and was accepted early to his dream school, Georgetown University.

Up until the day before January 1—when regular decision applications were due—Jacob was set on going to Georgetown. But on a whim, he sent in a second application to Yale—and much to his surprise, got in. He fell in love with the university later that spring during a tour of the campus.

Jacob is a tour guide himself now, as well as the chief of staff for Students for a New American Politics, America's only student-run political action committee. In 2018, the PAC funded forty-five low-income students from forty-four universities to work on selected campaigns throughout the country. A political science major, Jacob also dedicates time to political campaign volunteer work, Model UN conferences, and the New Haven Urban Debate League. In his free time, he likes to spend time with friends in Grace Hopper College, which he calls a particularly tight-knit residential college community.

Reflecting on his college admissions essay three years after writing it, Jacob says that going to Yale did, in fact, help him to expand his horizons beyond the perimeters of his small town—which honored him with the declaration of "Jacob Malinowski Day" the September of his junior year of high school for his representation of Greendale at Boys' State and Boys' Nation, civic leadership programs run by the American Legion. Overwhelmingly white and middle class, Greendale only exposed him to "one or two" perspectives on what it means to be a young person, Jacob says. At Yale, he counters, there are 5,400 unique perspectives of "so many cool people from across the country and across the world from so many different backgrounds."

But Yale has also altered Jacob's own perspective on his hometown and his feelings toward those who decide to follow their destiny and return to "the bubble."

"It still rings true in a certain sense that people from small white towns have a tendency to always come back and always have the same path, but when I reread [my essay], I guess I don't know if that's a bad thing, to live pretty simply," Jacob says. "Maybe it's not a bad thing to live a pretty good life and be proud of who you are."

Jacob's essays include his Common App personal statement.

ESSAY 1 (COMMON APP):
PERSONAL STATEMENT

Wisconsin is not an exciting state. My town is not big and exciting, nor full of opportunities. It's not small enough for everyone
to know each other and for everyone to have their role in the
community. It's a great place to grow up, don't get me wrong,
but there's nothing special about it. Greendale separates itself
from the real world. Actually, it's known as "the bubble" because
nothing bad can permeate it, and nothing ever leaves. In fact,
many families return here, generation after generation. My
children—and their children—are destined to live here. People
in Greendale are normal. Sure, they all have their own careers,
different family dynamics, and a variety of interests. But everyone in this town lives a very typical life. This is because Greendale is detached from reality. It is safe. My neighbors don't lock
their doors because they don't have to. Crime is very low; bad
things simply just don't happen. And this safety isn't just physical, it's also a feeling. People return to Greendale because there
is no risk involved here. They get a house on a quiet street and
work the same job for their entire life. They never need to step
outside their comfort zone. Many of the people they associate
with share the same views on religion, politics, and many other
topics. The chances of some catastrophe affecting them are so
low that they are basically nonexistent. It's this low-risk, echo
chamber environment that draws people into Greendale. The desire for a zero-failure place overpowers any qualms about never
having that huge success. But I've never been able to cope with
that feeling. I tried hard in school, participated in many activities,
and worked a few jobs to attempt to separate myself from the
normalcy and escape the destiny that is Greendale. Once the
questions about college started pouring in, I realized I wanted
to leave my home in order to further my global sense. That I
want to surround myself with people who also take risks and
want to see each other succeed as well as themselves. And
when people asked where I was applying to college, what I

said was not nearly as important as what I didn't say. I am not applying to University of Wisconsin–Madison. UW-Madison is the end goal for any student at my high school that shows any form of promise; many students only apply here. And UW–Madison is great, it's just not great for me. I believe many of my colleagues will go here because, once again, it's not a big risk. With their grades and extracurriculars, they could give plenty of elite schools a great application, but they will definitely get into UW–Madison. It's only about 80 miles from my high school, which is a quick drive home in case anything goes wrong. I don't want a security blanket because it's a limit on being extraordinary. It seems like such a silly struggle when you see citizens around the globe who attempt to fight hunger, poverty, war, and oppression. But there's no way those people can extricate themselves from conflict without the help of others. And how can I step up to that challenge if I settle and remain safe? This country wasn't built on caution and security, it was built on bravery and action. Brave people stood up for what they believed in and left their normal lives to pursue greatness. I do not strive to find the easiest way through my life; I want to escape this alleged "destiny." I believe I can pop the bubble that is Greendale and, with diligence, become a leader and find a meaning beyond my hometown.

Samantha Wood

Hometown: Wolfeboro, NH
Year: Sophomore
College: Saybrook
Major(s): Religious Studies
Extracurriculars: Yale Debate Association; Varsity Fencing

PROFILE

Samantha Wood, a Wolfeboro, New Hampshire, native, is a self-described "really typical nerd." Besides genuinely enjoying her classes, her high school activities included editing the literary magazine and competing on both the math and quiz bowl teams. Because her parents lacked access to education—her father didn't graduate high school but has a GED—they placed a high value on Samantha's education and academic achievements. Still, of all her activities in high school, Samantha was most proud of fencing. In her Common App essay, Samantha details her improvement and surmises that her fencing accomplishments brought her the most satisfaction because the sport, unlike her academic endeavors, did not come naturally to her at all. Describing her success on the fencing mat, Samantha conjures up a tangible sense of pride, but her modesty also bleeds through her words both about fencing and about her overall character. "I was good for my small town but I wasn't world quality in anything. I hadn't done anything earth-shattering by the time I got to Yale."

This modesty followed her to New Haven, where she hoped to continue the activities she was passionate about from high school while still expanding her horizons. Like many others, though, she feared she would not measure up to Yale's lofty standards. Luckily, Samantha's roommate convinced her to try out for the debate team, something she had wished to try despite having no prior experience. She recalls being so nervous she actually cried during her tryout, but she earned a spot on Yale's debate team that she still holds as a rising junior.

In the classroom, Samantha also made major changes to the plans she envisioned when she first arrived on campus. Because biology and chemistry classes had always interested Samantha in high school, she set out in the fall of her first year as an intended biochemistry major. Taking the intro courses at Yale, however, proved less enjoyable than she had imagined, so she decided to enroll in classes that had not been available to her through the New Hampshire public school system. Exposure to a wide variety of religious studies classes soon opened Samantha up to a new area of academic study, and she eventually switched gears to begin pursuing a major in religious studies.

When she first visited Yale with her mom, Samantha was surprised at how genuinely happy the students looked, even in the midst of finals. She knew she wanted to be part of a place that emphasized the importance of balance and individuality, and she made sure to demonstrate these qualities in herself for her application. Already boasting impressive grades and an array of extracurriculars, Samantha believes she stood out because her essays showed personality and a quirky, upbeat voice, two things she has continued to carry during her past two years in New Haven.

Samantha's essays include her Common App personal statement and one of her Yale supplemental essays.

ESSAY 1 (COMMON APP):
PERSONAL STATEMENT

The lessons we take from obstacles we encounter can be fundamental to later success. Recount a time when you faced a challenge, setback, or failure. How did it affect you, and what did you learn from the experience?

LOSING AND LIKING IT

When I first started competing nationally, I was a pretty dreadful fencer. At the tournament, many of the girls—who had trained since they were somewhere between zygotes and elementary school students—knew before they'd even started fencing for the day that they would beat at least one person: me. This was an unusual position for me to be in because I had become accustomed to winning, or at least coming close, in every endeavor, from the geography bee to games of cards. While some things remained stubbornly out of my reach, such as singing on key, writing in pen without always wishing that there was an eraser, and applying mascara without poking myself in the eye, most of the time when I tried something, I would succeed almost immediately.

When I failed, or rather, didn't succeed as much as I wanted, I would be quite upset with myself, wondering how I had misspelled a word so simple as "dimension" or missed a question on a math test. I knew that I was able to win and my inability to meet that potential disappointed me. Fencing, which required coordination, patience, and finesse, all things that I lacked, was the first endeavor in which I could initially expect nothing more from myself than losing with dignity.

I'd been competing for a year when I entered a large tournament in Kentucky, where I found myself fencing against the number one fencer in my age group. Tall, storm-eyed, and so fast that I didn't recognize that she was attacking before she'd already hit me, Morgan Partridge was so frightening that when I was called to fence against her, I laughed as one laughs at her own impending doom. In the next two minutes, she thwarted my best efforts to stop her unstoppable attacks and scored touches on me pretty much whenever the mood struck. That was why I was so surprised when I realized that my hand had twitched in just the right way and I had scored a touch on her. I felt the purest, most baffling sense of joy because, for a second, the impossible had happened; something worked for me.

Morgan won the bout 5 to 1. She flipped off her mask, threw back her blond ponytail, and let out a long, bone-rattling scream. As I shook her hand, I was still wondering how on earth I'd scored a touch on *the* Morgan Partridge. After the tournament, despite the fact that I had scored only eight touches all day, I couldn't stop smiling when I thought about my successful touches, though they were quite rare.

Learning that small victories hard earned are more valuable than blazing glory easily won was something I could only discover when I tried something that I had no natural talent for whatsoever. My fencing was painfully awkward; my coach called me "big brick" because of my slowness at learning new moves, my feet never seemed to move in the right direction and my ability to hit on target left plenty to be desired, yet I had never been happier.

Since that day in Kentucky, two years have passed. During that time, I fenced whenever my club was open, sometimes drilling actions with an endlessly patient teammate until our coach started jingling his keys and looking at the door. I entered every tournament I could and I was defeated both often and soundly. Agonizingly slowly, my victories became more common and less surprising. I started winning medals at local tournaments and my national results have become brilliantly mediocre. These are the things of which I am proudest. Though I have experienced greater success at school, I often discount these accomplishments because I know that they came easily. Fencing is the first thing in which I experienced failure and the thing from which I have gotten the most genuine joy. Satisfaction, I learned, doesn't come from accolades (though they are undoubtedly nice), but from improving through hard work.

ESSAY 2 (YALE SUPPLEMENT): PLEASE REFLECT ON SOMETHING YOU WOULD LIKE US TO KNOW ABOUT YOU THAT WE MIGHT NOT LEARN FROM THE REST OF YOUR APPLICATION, OR ON SOMETHING ABOUT WHICH YOU WOULD LIKE TO SAY MORE.

I love data sets almost as much as chocolate. Seeing the numbers lined up in columns, with their meaning desperate to be brought to light gives me a bit of a thrill. They remind me of the coloring books that well-meaning relatives give to children who display little artistic talent, in which the outlines on the pages are filled with vibrant colors when a thin layer of water is added to the paper. Data sets have that sort of meaning, only instead of water, statistical analysis must be brushed onto the pages.

When I received a packet telling me that I had been selected as a National Merit semifinalist, I was excited by the news itself, but what interested me even more were the pages following the announcement. Is there anything more tragic than an unexamined booklet of data points? They float around, directionless, with meanings that almost cry to be revealed. With a paper, a pencil, and a spreadsheet, I set out to discover what they were trying to say, amplifying the voices of the all-but-silent numbers.

There were the states and schools of all of the other semifinalists, ready to give up meaning to people who wanted to look. First I counted the number of homeschoolers and discovered that they made up about a third of a percent of all semifinalists, but 6 percent of all teenagers. Next I looked for the high schools with the largest percent of its students selected as scholars, and tried to find a reason why they had so many. In all, it was a pleasant afternoon. There were reasons, causes and effects hiding right below the surface, and I was the one to find them.

Holding the darling little data set on my lap, I watched as it took on different shapes with just a bit of coaxing. Each iteration revealed a small, beautiful truth about the world, one that may or may not have been seen before, but that was undeniably there. There was a beauty in unexpected outliers explained by further research. There was a feeling of intrepid exploration when faced with an uncharted data set. There was life in the numbers if you could overcome their soulless facade. The multitude of truths shimmered on the page like raindrops on a waxy leaf, ready to drip off with a gentle tap.

I occasionally try to share what I've found with my friends, who are now barely surprised when I mention that I analyzed a really great data set over the weekend. I'll share the most surprising things that I found from my analysis with them, then listen in turn as they tell me about their more eccentric tastes in clothing. We laugh, we smile, and we understand that it is unlikely that I'll ever comprehend how one of my dearest friends makes two different patterns complement each other. She'll never understand why the numbers make my heart flutter. There are some truths that cannot be found from data analysis, I suppose.

Juniors

James Barile

Hometown: Ridgefield, CT

Year: Junior

College: Pauli Murray

Major(s): Political Science

Extracurriculars: Lightweight Crew;
Yale Project Bright, president; Yale
Undergraduate Legal Aide Association,
founder

PROFILE

For James Barile, the most challenging aspect of the college application process was having to use the first-person "I" in his essays. "I think I wrote my applications on December 31 [the day before they were due]," he says, laughing, "because I didn't want to hear about myself and couldn't fathom that anyone else wanted to." James, who grew up in Ridgefield, Connecticut, recalls feeling that the strong focus on self-promotion throughout the college process often seemed "absolutely irreconcilable with all that I'd been raised to believe at the time."

Perhaps it's no surprise, then, that when James arrived at Yale, he found that he tended to most admire not the students and faculty who performed best academically, but those who excelled in other arenas at Yale—specifically those who made a point of giving back to their communities. As a result, James says, he has also prioritized "the immense resources at Yale for service work and far beyond that" during his years at the university.

A member of Pauli Murray College, James serves as the president of Yale Project Bright, an initiative that aims to increase the amount of solar energy generated by Yale. During his tenure, the project received seed funding from Tesla to expand solar energy to thirty private homes. James also helped start (and then led) the Yale Undergraduate Legal Aid Association, which provides free legal services to people in the Greater New Haven Area who are threatened by detention or otherwise ensnared in the immigration legal process.

James remembers having to choose on several occasions during his sophomore year "between going home and doing a problem set or calling a detained family . . . in Texas, to counsel them on their right to asylum." However, James adds that for him, "it was always a simple choice, and [the answer] wasn't academics."

Not all of James's activities at Yale are quite so high-stakes, however; as a member of the crew team, James also mentions that many of his favorite memories from the university involved time spent with his teammates, gliding down rivers on beautiful afternoons. Other favorite encounters include giving a piggyback ride to a professor's daughter right before going onto a Ferris wheel at the Guilford Fair—an experience he calls "surreal."

James's essays include two of his Yale supplemental essays.

ESSAY 1 (YALE SUPPLEMENT): WHAT IN PARTICULAR ABOUT YALE HAS INFLUENCED YOUR DECISION TO APPLY?

One hundred and twenty-five years ago, my great-grandfather watched his Nile crops wither. With every drop of talent I've been endowed, I seek to clean the rivers into which he wept.

The dialectic acuteness of student research at Yale's School of Forestry (ie Prof. Shimon Anisfeld's sediment fingerprinting for East African watershed) and breadth in the humanities suits this end.

Yet I crave Yalies too: meaningful and intimate exchanges with classmates (per residential colleges) who, like me, hang their cleats above a copy of Plato's Republic—and with professors (by lunch, co-authorship, or Master's Tea) impelled by one lodestar across many skies.

That is Yale.

ESSAY 2 (YALE SUPPLEMENT): SHORT TAKES

You have been granted a free weekend next month. How will you spend it?

Mitigating erosion with a friend at Bennett's Pond State Park, while playing an analogy game (e.g. proton : clock = relative : proportional motion)

What is something about which you have changed your mind in the last three years?

A perpetual high note becomes no sound at all; low notes make the music. (Adversities should be embraced, not feared/ hidden, for our limits define us)

What is the best piece of advice you have received while in high school?

"Jump." (Standing on an iceberg over a 38-degree glacial lake in the Grand Tetons. I did.)

What do you wish you were better at being or doing?

Fluent in more languages. Language is the currency of thought, and thought governs our mind, so I think monolingualism prelimited my human experience.

What is a learning experience, in or out of the classroom, that has had a significant impact on you?

At UChi Summer School, taking a coffee break at 1 a.m., and ending up talking with a 20-something for ½ hr on a bus about why he carried a gun (Pride).

Haci Catalbasoglu

Hometown: New Haven, CT

Year: Junior

College: Davenport

Major(s): Political Science

Extracurriculars: New Haven Ward 1
Alderman (New Haven Board of Alders)

PROFILE

Born and raised in New Haven, Hacibey (Haci) Catalbasoglu is the city's youngest ever representative to the Board of Alders—New Haven's legislative arm. As Ward 1 alder, Haci represents the only all-Yale ward of the city, and works to improve the town-gown relationship between the university and the Elm City.

Haci is a political science major with a concentration in urban studies. His father, a Turkish immigrant, is the owner and operator of Brick Oven Pizza in downtown New Haven. Before graduating high school, Haci spent many days and nights working at his father's small business, often serving Yale students, professors, and staff. Haci is the first in his family to attend college, and he grew up with the philosophy that if you want to do something—no matter how outlandish it may seem—it is achievable.

Upon arriving at Yale, Haci knew that his goal was to figure out what his passion was, and he knew that the only way he could really do that was by "trying everything." Along with joining clubs and meeting new people, Haci walked onto the heavyweight crew team the year they won the national championship. He went from an "average athlete" to rowing next to future Olympians at Yale.

But Haci says that the most invaluable thing Yale has given him is the desire to learn. He attended a high school where, to most, academics were not a priority; Haci didn't have a longing to learn and didn't enjoy spending his days in a classroom. However, this completely changed once he arrived at Yale. Whether the topic is "municipal finance or Greek history," whenever something piques his interest, Haci tries to learn more about it, simply because it brings him joy.

Haci knew that going to Yale would involve a rigorous academic life, but that's not where he cites his most valuable experiences. Haci's personal growth has taken place late at night in his suite's common room, discussing global politics with his suitemates and in the process of launching his alderman campaign.

Haci says that these kinds of experiences offer a unique type of learning that one wouldn't be able to find elsewhere. What makes Yale so special, according to Haci, is the environment outside of the classroom, which allows students to test their limits and discover things that one wouldn't necessarily learn from a textbook.

Haci's essays include his Common App personal statement.

ESSAY 1 (COMMON APP):
PERSONAL STATEMENT

THAT KID FROM BRICK OVEN

I was five years old when my immigrant father created a makeshift bed out of two blankets from his truck and proceeded to put it under a brick oven for me sleep in. It was 2 a.m. on a Saturday night and I was exhausted, so my father's most practical solution was for me to sleep under the oven. I remember thinking to myself, "What the heck am I doing here?"

At the time, my parents were newly divorced, and I stayed with my father during the weekends. Because we did not have a babysitter, I was stuck at my father's late-night restaurant, the Brick Oven Pizza, every weekend from 3 p.m. to 3 a.m.

Working at his restaurant in downtown New Haven, CT for nearly my entire life, I envied my friends who were at home playing video games and living normal kid lives. While they were challenging goblins and beating strange characters, I was challenging wood in a brick oven and beating dough on a granite counter. One time, to entertain myself, I tied three Coke bottles to a bucket and shook it to see if it would reach the moon. It didn't, but I did learn a couple of things: making a soda rocket is very messy, and that three bottles aren't enough. In hindsight, it was probably a good learning experience, because with any messier experimentation, I might have learned what pizza dough felt like after being pounded by the hands of my father.

By the time I was ten, I could take orders on the phone and operate the register. Although I had to stand on a chair to see the person on the other side of the counter, I did my job, and I did it well. By twelve, I managed and worked full-time during weekends and summers at the Brick Oven. While manning the register, I met a variety of people—young and old, rich and poor, patient and impatient alike. On a typical night, I had conversations with everyone from giggling girls at 2 a.m. who just got out of the nearby nightclub, to Yale professors who stopped by to buy a slice, to (Bad) Chad Dawson, a New Haven native and boxing champion. I fell in love with talking and interacting with people, and people fell in love with my corny icebreakers.

Over the years I've learned so much from this restaurant in downtown New Haven and its community. I have met so many people that wherever I go, I'm referred to as "that kid from Brick Oven." In the countless hours spent at what is essentially my second home, I learned, firsthand, how to be an accountant, a behavioral therapist, a manager, a baker, a handyman, a social worker, and a skilled multi-tasker, all at the same time. I know that I will learn much more in college, but I anticipate that these skills will also come in handy. Most importantly, however, I witnessed my immigrant father working tirelessly throughout the years to support and build a life for me in the United States. The message I constantly heard from him was, "Son, work hard in school, so that you won't have to work like me." With this, his blue-collar work ethic was, and still is, instilled in me.

I never did get an Xbox or PlayStation, but it did not matter because I had my powdery flour, my cash register, and my friends from all over New Haven. I had the opportunity to learn fast from my surroundings, not just how to spin a perfect crust, but also how to interact with all sorts of people, at their best and their worst, at every hour of night. Most of all, I'm excited to explore what's on the other side of the counter and what new challenges are in store for me in the future.

Louis DeFelice

Hometown: Columbia, SC

Year: Junior

College: Jonathan Edwards

Major(s): English

Extracurriculars: Tour guide; songwriting

PROFILE

In high school, Louis DeFelice was first and foremost a dancer. He attended the South Carolina Governor's School, a public boarding school for the arts, and trained in ballet. There, he also became interested in personal finance; in his senior year, he started reading books about investment to figure out how to handle the leftover money saved up from his dishwashing job. Ultimately, this led Louis to start WonderLearnInvest .com, a website for sharing tips on smart money-saving.

Halfway through his senior year of high school, Louis left the Governor's School to train in ballet privately. He took a gap year, focusing on his dancing career and learning how to live independently, and ultimately received his high school diploma from an online school.

Louis was most attracted to Yale because of its curious, motivated students and the intellectual stimulation he knew he'd find there. "The financial, physical, mentorship, and human capital capacity of Yale is very high," he remarks. "People are very generous with their time."

Louis adds that he is especially appreciative of the social communities he's found at Yale. He remembers that during his sophomore and junior years, when he underwent some difficulties in his personal life, he received an outpouring of support from friends as well as professors, who were often forgiving when he had to miss class meetings and were willing to lend a listening ear at their office hours. At that time, Louis also learned to take advantage of mental health and counseling resources on campus.

At Yale, Louis has worked as a tour guide for the admissions office, performed as a member of Tangled Up in Blue—a folk music singing group— and produced original music in the Jonathan Edwards recording studio. Some of his favorite memories at Yale include playing gigs with his band at local venues, where he loves the energetic vibe and the enthusiasm of the audience. After graduation, he plans to live in New York and pursue a career in music.

Louis's essays include his Common App personal statement.

ESSAY 1 (COMMON APP):
PERSONAL STATEMENT
Discuss an accomplishment or event, formal or informal, that marked your transition from childhood to adulthood within your culture, community, or family.

I grew up in Columbia, S.C., but I moved away from home as a sophomore to go to a residential high school for the arts. Doing so gave me more independence than any of my peers or I had ever had. Until a few months ago, I would have said that moving away was my most significant transition toward adulthood; however, I realized a greater level of independence during the summer of 2013. I spent the month of June living with two other boys in an apartment in Salt Lake City. I flew to Utah on my own to dance on scholarship with Ballet West, and living there was the first time that I had been completely without the supervision of parents or teachers. From auditioning and meeting the director in March, to flying across the country on my own, it was a new and transformative experience, and one that I undertook on my own. I saved money, shopped for groceries, cooked my meals, and used buses and trains to get to class and rehearsal every day. I had the freedom to travel around the city at my leisure, but it was also up to me to get to class on time, take care of the apartment, etc. Although I've lived in a dorm since I was fifteen, the level of responsibility that I had in Utah was very different from what I was used to at the Governor's School, especially the absence of curfews, cafeterias, and supervision. That, however, was only half of my summer. After I left Salt Lake City, I went to London to dance at the Royal Ballet School. I stayed with a host mother who provided my meals, but I was completely responsible for using public transportation to get across the city to school each day. Being able to spend my evenings and weekends sightseeing and exploring London with friends, or on my own, was incredible. The experiences that I had in London, and Salt Lake City, were formative and I feel that I accomplished what I hoped to in both places. The opportunities that I had to train with no many teachers and coaches was remarkable, but the time that I spent in each city, and the people that I spent it with, were equally influential. The independence was endlessly exciting, and the adventures that I had this summer taught me a lot about myself. I enjoyed meeting different people from around the world, and learning about their cultures, which were both so similar to and different from my own. In London, I loved going to lunch with three or four other dancers and having conversations that would involve five different languages. Being able to hear and practice foreign languages inspired me, and drove me to work harder at becoming multilingual. Experiencing so many new things, both in and out of my classes, required me to mature quickly and work hard, but also helped to shape my goals for the future, specifically what I want to study for the next several years.

Nick Girard

Hometown: Stafford Springs, CT

Year: Junior

College: Ezra Stiles

Major(s): Political Science

Extracurriculars: Yale College Council, vice president; College Democrats of Connecticut, president

PROFILE

Politics has been a passion since high school for Nick Girard, who views public service as an effective means of becoming truly engaged with his community. Politics has shaped Nick's trajectory at Yale—he served as vice president of the Yale College Council and president of the College Democrats of Connecticut—and still informs his career choices as he completes his senior year.

As a first-generation college student from a small town in northern Connecticut, Nick initially felt overwhelmed with the different opportunities presented to him at Yale. He didn't know how to access most of the resources offered on campus. "Coming to Yale the first few weeks, I had a lot of doubts and concerns about whether I would be able to fit in at this school that attracts the best and the brightest from around the world," Nick recalls. That kind of experience transformed the rest of his career at Yale: from that point on, he said, he resolved to make Yale a more accessible and welcoming environment for everyone.

Nick's efforts to make Yale more accessible culminated last school year with his election as vice president of the Yale College Council. His proudest accomplishment, the launch of the Domestic Summer Award, has also been a personal one, Nick said. The new fellowship, which provides students with funding for summer opportunities at nonprofits and government organizations, opens doors for students who would not otherwise be able to afford to take unpaid summer jobs like internships at the Senate or art apprenticeships, he explains. "The award will make a lasting change on what people will be able to do at Yale—and based on that, what they will be able to do far beyond Yale."

Nick's experiences at Yale with politics also extend to the Yale College Democrats, an organization that has not only become a tight-knit community for him, but has also expanded his horizons. Nick explained that he never would have believed, prior to Yale, that he would be able to meet with former Secretary of State Hillary Clinton or former Governor Dannel Malloy of Connecticut as a college student, but his involvement in the Yale College Democrats made those meetings possible. These experiences exemplify his belief that Yale is a place where people can surprise themselves by unlocking newfound potential, as long as they have the right support system and a welcoming environment around them.

Nick is a first-year counselor during his senior year, helping fresh faces in Ezra Stiles College get acclimated to Yale. He hopes to draw upon his own experiences as a first-year, when he first felt out of place at Yale. Ultimately, Nick wants to make an impact by helping others find their own communities, as he did with the Yale College Council and the Yale College Democrats. "The beauty of Yale is that there are just so many ways in which you can leave your mark," he reflects.

Nick's essays include his Common App personal statement and one of his Yale supplemental essays.

ESSAY 1 (COMMON APP):
PERSONAL STATEMENT

Some students have a background or story that is so central to their identity that they believe their application would be incomplete without it. If this sounds like you, then please share your story.

The temperature reaches the single digits, but my heart is on fire because it is Election Day 2013 and I am ready for action. I grab my campaign signs, my mittens, and my homemade campaign buttons and head out. It is 5 a.m. and there is no one out except for the small group at headquarters. As the sun starts to rise and the cars start to roll by, more volunteers show up. I begrudgingly agree that I have to go to school, but my mind begs: "Ten more minutes?" At school, it seems I am the only one excited. It puzzles me because these elections are, for most of us, one of the few opportunities to influence the decisions that govern our community. Soon, I find myself back at headquarters, which is now abuzz as "election day fever" sets in. I make calls throughout the afternoon as we see more signs of a low voter turnout. Politics has taught me persistence and the value of never giving up on something. On a campaign, don't just accept that voters are not turning up; call them, remind them that their vote counts, listen to them when they say why they aren't voting, and offer a solution. The sun sets and the numbers start to roll in. We make a crowd now. Our candidates are here, signs are everywhere, and voter call sheets are strewn about the room. In the end, our candidate lost the First Selectman race, but we managed to fill most other positions.

It was an unmatchable experience to help the Stafford Democratic Town Committee in our 2013 municipal campaign, and Election Day was my favorite. The excitement was real and so was the disappointment. I feel at home at headquarters and each visit reinforces that this is where I am meant to be. In the anticipation waiting for the results to come in, the feeling of perfect content, like a puzzle piece finally fitting in, occurred. I at once felt an incredible sense of pride, but also a great weight of responsibility. Politics and government have become the air I breathe and my lifelong passion. Every day is another chance to reach more people, to do more good, and, little by little, to change the world. I always knew I enjoyed politics, and fondly remember saving up as a six-year-old to buy a poster of presidents that still hangs on my wall. Until last year, I never thought I could be where I am today and didn't dream as big and strategize so seriously about what I can be in the future. In a world full of change, that presidents poster, and my commitment to politics, remain a sturdy foundation for the future. From the High School Democrats of America to the Connecticut Democratic Party, that one short election in 2013 marked a great impetus for my future in public service and politics. I felt content, rewarded, and passionate working side-by-side with our candidates.

Political work is tremendously difficult, but it is rewarding and pays in the knowledge of the skills needed to be a successful public leader: a clear vision, commitment to community, tenacity, and passion. Each day on the campaign trail, incredible stories of determination, compassion, and concern are shared. Politics to me is more than the negative ads and mudslinging; it is the opportunity to gain a better understanding and recognition of the incredible diversity of experiences and opinions in this world. The world needs devoted, dedicated, and compassionate individuals who can be the agents of change and progress for the future. I know I can be one.

ESSAY 2 (YALE SUPPLEMENT): IN THIS ESSAY, PLEASE REFLECT ON SOMETHING YOU WOULD LIKE US TO KNOW ABOUT YOU THAT WE MIGHT NOT LEARN FROM THE REST OF YOUR APPLICATION, OR ON SOMETHING ABOUT WHICH YOU WOULD LIKE TO SAY MORE.

My journey to become the kind of leader I strive to be started with a regret and resulted in me learning to value every opportunity I am given. In 2011, I attended a leadership seminar through the Student Leadership Training Program. Despite the eye-opening experience, I was not ready to apply new leadership skills and stay involved. I was handed a tremendous experience, and in the naivety of my caged mind, I neglected to take advantage of it like a bird fearing to take flight for the risk of falling.

With sophomore year came a new opportunity—I received the Hugh O'Brian Youth Leadership Award and was asked to attend the Connecticut Hugh O'Brian Youth Leadership Conference. This would be my second chance to learn from a leadership conference. I promised to not let this experience fall through my fingers. Initially, I was intimidated, with strange "Outstanding" cheers and experiences that were miles out of my comfort zone. I felt out of place. Why did I deserve to be here? I had given up on my previous commitments, while other ambassadors were devoted, accomplished leaders.

Over the weekend though, something in me clicked, and my apprehension disappeared. I realized who I am and how I can contribute to the world. When pushed beyond my limits socially, intellectually, and mentally, I found a learning experience unrivaled by anything thus far in my life.

A leader is not just the person in front of the line, the person who is the loudest, or the one who has the most to say. Leadership to me is the power to thrive in any circumstance, to lead through service, and to empower others. A true commitment to something greater than oneself takes great devotion. A leader listens to the concerns, hopes, and dreams of everyone and uses words and actions to encourage others. During seminar this year, we visited with senior residents, and I met a man who was a judge and leader in his community many years ago but could now barely speak. I told him about HOBY's impact on me and he listened contently. I apologized at the end because I thought I bored him, but he smiled. "Be exactly who you are, do not change," he told me. That moment reassured me of everything HOBY has awoken in me. New experiences, disappointments, triumphs, and everyday life experiences help to mold a leader. Each day we have choices to make. Each choice is an opportunity to build character and create positive change. A leader strives to makes the right choices, recognizes and addresses mistakes, and motivates others. When I think about what is important to me, I think about my experiences that have taught me to push the boundaries of my capabilities, embrace new experiences, and do the right thing instead of the easy thing. I don't have all of the answers, but these skills will help me become the person and leader I want to be.

Tony Grant

Hometown: Hyannis, MA

Year: Junior

College: Silliman

Major(s): Political Science

Extracurriculars: Eli Whitney Students Society, co-president; Yale Student Veterans Council, president; Yale Veterans Association, vice president; IRIS; long-distance bicycling

PROFILE

Tony Grant applied to Yale understanding that his application showed an unconventional path to New Haven. Tony—a Massachusetts native whose father served in the navy throughout his childhood—matriculated at Yale through the Eli Whitney Students Program. EWSP is an admissions program for undergraduate applicants who have had their education interrupted for five or more years. Previously, Tony served in the U.S. Air Force for seven years—first as an Arabic translator, then as a crisis manager, coordinating support for U.S. operations.

After graduating from high school in Mississippi, where his father's service had brought the family, Tony studied at the Mississippi Gulf Coast Community College with a full scholarship. Although he spent only a year there before leaving to join the military, he always intended to finish his undergraduate degree later in life.

Yale's residential college system, often the linchpin of

students' social experience, impacts Tony and other Eli Whitney students only tangentially, since they do not live on campus. Although Tony is affiliated with Silliman College, he lives in East Rock with his wife of seven years, who is currently a social worker in the area. Together, they have built a life that centers around Tony's ability to complete his degree.

Students who live on campus or in downtown New Haven live and study in the same area, but Tony has to commute to and from class by bike every day. This forces him to separate his home and school life and be more deliberate about his on-campus plans. Socially, outside of the Eli Whitney cohort, which Tony describes as "real tight," he initially struggled, lacking an immediate group of close-knit Yale friends as well as structures like the first-year counselor system that most students take for granted. Instead, both in the Air Force and now as a student, Tony has credited religion for his ability to face the challenges and quirks presented by his unconventional path.

Within and alongside his political science major, Tony studies health economics and public policy and hopes to work in that field following his graduation.

Tony's essays include his Eli Whitney Students Program essay.

ESSAY 1 (ELI WHITNEY STUDENTS PROGRAM): WHAT ARE YOUR REASONS FOR APPLYING TO THE ELI WHITNEY STUDENTS PROGRAM AT YALE? WHAT PERSONAL AND ACADEMIC GOALS DO YOU THINK YALE CAN HELP YOU REACH?

When I compiled a list of realistic colleges to attend this fall, Yale did not find a spot on it. In my mind, I did not have the GPA, ACT score, or spotless background leaving high school to belong there. Truth be told, I relinquished the idea when I got my first "B–." It wasn't until a Service to School ambassador mentioned Eli Whitney students in passing and said that I should look into it. With a healthy amount of skepticism, I scrolled through the student profiles thinking that I would find a gallery of innovators and geniuses. On the contrary, I repeatedly saw normal, driven people who simply didn't finish their four-year degree on their anticipated schedule. I was convinced that Yale is offering a second chance to hardworking students who have taken the less-traveled path to college. Therefore, I'm applying to the Eli Whitney Students program to take the once-in-a-lifetime chance to study International Relations at a school with a historic record of excellence that would not have been an option for me before I enlisted in the Air Force.

Completing my undergraduate studies at Yale means more to me than having a selective school attached to my name; It means taking advantage of the opportunity to academically flourish among Yale's collaborative, high-energy faculty and student body. I plan to spend hours with Dr. Muhammad Aziz and the rest of the department working to attain a greater grasp on Modern Standard Arabic and build upon its dialects that I labored so arduously to refine. I also hope to supplement my area-specific language study with a secondary language in either French or German. Overall, my most ambitious academic goal is to find a logical and unbiased voice to offer solutions on international topics. The renowned Jackson Institute for Global Affairs can help me bridge the gap between in-depth academia and the military-specific knowledge that I gained in the intelligence field to create a more comprehensive view of global affairs. I believe it is necessary to mature out of my niche perspective of the world and to fairly analyze contemporary issues in a future career.

Outside of academics, my personal aspirations gravitate toward veterans advocacy and foreign cultures. I've received so much crucial advice and encouragement throughout my career from others that have served, and I want to do what I can to see Yale's student veteran community strengthen and expand. At the same time, Yale's diversity offers the perfect environment to interact first-hand with representatives of the world that I dream of visiting.

Jacob Hillman

Hometown: Plano, TX

Year: Junior

College: Berkeley

Major(s): Computer Science

Extracurriculars: Yale Concert Band;
Jazz Band

PROFILE

"I was definitely not considering Yale in high school," says Jacob Hillman, who transferred to Yale in 2017 from Southern Methodist University in Dallas. Jacob grew up in Plano, Texas, and attended a "massive public school" with a graduating class of about fifteen hundred students. Most of his classmates elected to stay in Texas for college.

"I wasn't valedictorian or anything like that," Jacob said. "At the time I thought there was no way I would get into Yale, so it just didn't even cross my mind to apply."

At SMU, Jacob double majored in computer science and music, often taking seven or eight classes per semester. On a typical day, his classes and band rehearsals took up his entire day. He wouldn't start on his homework until the evening. Meanwhile, Jacob says, most of his classmates found a lot more time for fun as they took on lighter class schedules.

It did not occur to Jacob that he could transfer schools until he visited Yale. During his sophomore year at SMU, he stayed with a friend in Morse College at Yale. They enjoyed a comedy show, jazz band rehearsal, and a score of get-togethers in the residential college.

"I discovered, like, holy cow . . . at some point in my life I need to go to Yale," Jacob said. At first, Jacob thought that might mean graduate school. But then a Yale student asked if he was transferring, and Jacob seriously considered the option.

Yale was the only college Jacob applied to as a transfer student. "If I got in, I would go; if not, I was fine to stay at SMU," he said.

Now a senior at Yale, Jacob affirmed, "Yale has completely exceeded my expectations, and I just could not be happier."

Jacob majors in computer science—he shed the double major to allow for a more varied course load at Yale—and divvies his time outside class between a quintet of extracurriculars: Yale Concert Band; Yale Jazz Ensemble; a saxophone quartet; Code Haven, a program where Yale students teach middle schoolers how to code; and Matriculate, a nonprofit organization that pairs underprivileged high schoolers with college students to help them through the college admissions process. When he gets a spare moment, Jacob loves to take photographs, a hobby that he took up in high school but continues to pursue in his free time. He hopes to showcase a collection of black-and-white portraits of fellow transfer students in an exhibition before he graduates.

The busy schedule can be deceiving, however.

"Sometimes it feels like I was working harder at SMU," Jacob remarks. "I'm happier to be doing the things that I'm involved in at Yale, so I don't necessarily feel like I'm working as hard."

When asked about his favorite memory at Yale so far, Jacob describes Pierson Inferno, a university-sponsored Halloween party in Pierson College. Jacob, sporting a baby costume complete with a pacifier and a teddy-bear-patterned bonnet, spent the night dancing and chatting with friends. He says he had no idea that there were colleges where one could expect great community turnout and enthusiasm for a such a quirky, school-sponsored event.

Jacob's essays include two of his transfer student application essays and four Yale supplemental essays.

ESSAY 1 (TRANSFER-SPECIFIC YALE SUPPLEMENT): WHAT IS A COMMUNITY TO WHICH YOU BELONG? REFLECT ON THE FOOTPRINT THAT YOU HAVE LEFT.

"I felt disconnected, and that Ware Residential Commons wasn't anything close to the community I was expecting. I thought the residential commons system was a hoax." I paused after this statement, and looked up to see 120 pairs of nervous, confused freshman eyes pondering my last statement. I stood behind the podium, still confident that this statement was a good decision.

Living in Ware, one of the eleven Residential Commons on SMU's campus, challenged me to recognize what it means to be part of a community. I noticed a lack of community in the Commons, so I ran for and became president of the Ware Commons Council. My goal was to create an environment everyone was proud to call "home."

Every day, I am actively trying to make Ware a stronger community, and the goal of my speech to the incoming freshmen was to inspire them to want to do the same. I have seen and felt improvements in the strength of our community. A nervous, Indian American resident and approached me and said, "Jacob, I just want to say thank you. Coming here, I was nervous I wasn't going to fit in. But you've made me feel like I belong here. Thank you."

ESSAY 2 (YALE SUPPLEMENT): WRITE ABOUT SOMETHING THAT YOU LOVE TO DO.

"3, 2, 1 . . ." I gently pull my finger down on the shutter, careful not to let the camera move in the precious 1/500 of a second the sensor is exposed to light. I then quickly press the shutter a few more times, with the hope of accidentally capturing a slight sense of relief, or maybe even a snicker of laughter. I look down at the preview on the small screen, and my heart starts to race a little. The lighting is *just* right—soft and white, but with warm bokeh radiating behind the subject's profile. I turn the camera around, and the subject loves it. They then turn themselves around, not quite sure of how this picture resulted from the seemingly average setting we are in. But that's why I love photography—there is hidden potential everywhere. If I crank down the aperture to f1.8, opening the sensor up to as much light as possible, I can turn tall blades of grass into a beautifully textured backdrop. I can turn water falling onto a rock into an explosion of reflective color. Photography is more than just capturing a moment in time—it's an opportunity for both interpretation and expression.

ESSAY 3 (YALE SUPPLEMENT): WHAT IN PARTICULAR ABOUT YALE HAS INFLUENCED YOUR DECISION TO APPLY?

"Do we really need to get there early?" I asked my friend, a current Yale student, in reference to a student comedy show that was going to be performed in Saybrook College's Underbrook theater on Yale's campus. There's *no* way this thing will fill up, I thought. My doubts were quickly dispersed as we approached the theater—there was a line of eager students looped throughout the basement halls. After the show, I totally understood why the demand was so great. These students were incredibly talented, and the show was hilarious. This event is a physical representation of the vibe I got on campus both times I visited. Yale is a collection of talented, brilliant, and diverse students who support each other, building a strong community unlike any other. Everyone at Yale seems to have a place. Yale provides resources to help students succeed, but there is a mutualistic relationship—the students are what make Yale so special. When I'm on campus at Yale, I feel inspired—inspired to pursue what I'm passionate about, and inspired to help others around me do the same. I want to share my talents with the community and support my peers who want to do the same.

ESSAY 4 (TRANSFER-SPECIFIC YALE SUPPLEMENT): PLEASE PROVIDE A STATEMENT THAT ADDRESSES YOUR REASONS FOR TRANSFERRING AND THE OBJECTIVES YOU HOPE TO ACHIEVE.

I'm extremely passionate about everything I am doing at SMU. The opportunity to double major in music and computer science has challenged me academically at an exceedingly high level. A great characteristic about the experience at SMU is that the student can determine what kind of college experience they want to have. At SMU, I have been able to discover that I want the most academic experience possible.

All together, SMU has done an amazing job providing me with opportunities, both academic and extracurricular. There is nothing at SMU stopping me from pursuing what I'm passionate about, and I am especially thankful for the unforgettable relationships I have been able to establish with my professors and mentors. However, I feel like there is more that I can do, and more that I can give. I want to be pushed even harder so that I can live up to more of my potential. While I have nothing but absolute admiration and appreciation for those who have taught me at SMU, I am also excited by the thought of interacting and making connections with the professors at Yale. I have learned a significant amount through mentorship relationships I've sought out, and believe the relationships I could build at Yale would be the strongest and most influential to date.

I am in a unique period of my life where I can surround myself with people my age who share a similar level of passion as me. After visiting Yale, I noticed an inspiration coming from the students around me that, up to that point, I had not experienced at SMU. I realized that I am one of the few choosing to have such an academically challenging experience here on campus. When I visited Yale, I sat in on classes and a jazz band rehearsal, had a valuable conversation with the Director of Bands, and watched a student-run comedy show. Even after leaving Yale's campus, I remembered what I witnessed about the students and level of academic rigor, and was motivated to work even harder to accomplish my goals back at SMU for a few weeks to follow. I also remembered the connection I felt to the students that I met on campus, instantly strengthened by our common goals and appreciation of the education they are getting. The combination of increased opportunity, higher expectations, and unparalleled inspiration lead me to believe I can accomplish the most I am capable of at Yale.

At Yale, I would hope to continue studying both computer science and music. I have been in contact with Carrie Koffman, the Lecturer in Saxophone at Yale. This is the first year that Yale has ever had a sax program, and I hope to bring my two years of experience as a music major at a rigorous music school, where I play Principal Saxophone in the top Wind Ensemble, to this young studio. I plan to play in the Yale Concert Band, Yale Jazz Ensemble, and a saxophone quartet.

ESSAY 5 (YALE SUPPLEMENT): IF YOU SELECTED ONE OF THE COMPUTER SCIENCE OR ENGINEERING MAJORS, PLEASE TELL US MORE ABOUT WHAT HAS LED YOU TO AN INTEREST IN THIS FIELD OF STUDY, WHAT EXPERIENCES (IF ANY) YOU HAVE HAD IN COMPUTER SCIENCE OR ENGINEERING, AND WHAT IT IS ABOUT YALE'S PROGRAM IN THIS AREA THAT APPEALS TO YOU.

Throughout my life, I have naturally gravitated toward creative problem solving and critical thinking. I have scored in the 99th percentile for cognitive abilities, and pride myself in my ability to quickly pick up on new concepts. I figured that a path in engineering would most closely fit my skills and interests, however I had no idea what exactly I wanted to do within the discipline. I ended up picking mechanical engineering for its "broadness," but made sure to go to a school that would facilitate a switch into another area of study. I took my first computer science class during my second semester at SMU—Introduction to Java. Both excited and slightly intimidated by the breadth of this new domain I was entering, I soon realized I had an aptitude for computer science. At the end of the semester, I created a culminating project called "improWise." My goal for this project was to develop a program that allows inexperienced musicians to easily create simple improvised melodies over a looping chord progression. The summer after my freshman year, I took an intense and comprehensive C++ class in Weimar, Germany with Mark Fontenot, a professor from SMU. After this class, which solidified my interest and passion for computer science, and at the urging of my Java professor, I switched my major to Computer Science.

As my experience and technical ability in computer science continues to grow, I am beginning to identify the true potential within the field. A huge area of interest for me is the collaboration between music and computer science. An example of this collaboration that I have recently discovered is the idea of algorithmic composition. As a music major, I have taken many Music Theory classes, and have a very solid understanding of the mechanics and "language" of music. I believe this understanding is essential in programming a system to compose and create music. Yale has shown remarkable progress in this field through Euterpea and the Yale Haskell Group and, more than any other school, would encourage this exploration and provide me with the best opportunities to explore this realm.

In addition, Yale's largely theoretical and mathematical approach to computer science would give me a broad understanding of the field, allowing for a wide range of opportunities and applications after graduation. Because computer science is such a fast moving field, this fundamental understanding would be particularly valuable.

I have complete confidence in my ability to succeed and excel in the academic environment that Yale offers. The environment that Yale offers would give me the space and the tools to both excel in the classroom and pursue my personal interests and passions.

ESSAY 6 (YALE SUPPLEMENT): WHY DO THESE AREAS APPEAL TO YOU? (COMPUTER SCIENCE, MUSIC)

"You're a magician," my friend once stated after I helped her understand one of her first Java programs. Looking back, I remember having the same thought as I watched someone program for the first time. My complete lack of understanding on the subject sparked a deep curiosity, an unquenchable thirst for knowledge.

Much earlier in my life, when I first picked up a saxophone, I remember it felt unnatural. I felt hundreds of mechanisms flexing uneasily under my fingers, and I couldn't make a sound. I was overcome with a similar curiosity.

I am passionate about building my vocabulary and proficiency in these areas, increasing my ability to express myself through creation. I want to become the best "magician" in the world.

Bri Matusovsky

Hometown: Los Angeles, CA

Year: Junior

College: Pierson

Major(s): Ecology & Evolutionary Biology

Extracurriculars: Voke Spoken Word;
Bad Romantics of Yale

PROFILE

During their senior year of high school, Bri Matusovsky—who uses *they/them/their* pronouns—received two life-changing surprises in just one day. On that fateful afternoon, Bri sat alone in their apartment when smoke began pouring out of a wall. After exiting the building, Bri watched as fire crews arrived and their family's home went up in flames.

But six hours later, they opened an online portal to find another surprise, this one much more pleasant: Their acceptance to Yale University. As a low-income student, Bri knew from early on in their high school career that acceptance to a top-tier, need-blind institution would mean paying no tuition. That factor, along with Yale's size, sense of community, strong STEM programs, and liberal arts-based structure made Yale Bri's ideal college. And in that moment, attending Yale became a reality.

"I never thought I was going to get in," Bri says. "Yale was just like a unicorn."

Growing up in West Hollywood, which has a large Eastern European immigrant community, Bri spoke exclusively

Russian at home and in the community they grew up in. They later attended a Russian preschool, and only moved to an English-speaking school for elementary school.

During high school, Bri volunteered at the nonprofit No Limits for Deaf Children; played water polo for two years, until they quit due to bullying; and participated in student government, in which they—despite facing yet more bullying—eventually became student body president.

At Yale, Bri is majoring in Ecology & Evolutionary Biology, works at the Connecticut Agricultural Experiment Station conducting mosquito research and has found the strong community ties they sought when looking for a college. They helped found Voke Spoken Word—a poetry group for LGBTQ students and allies—in their sophomore year and joined the Bad Romantics of Yale, a drag troupe that was "formative" for Bri in their journey of self-acceptance and self-love.

"Yale has proven to me to be a place where, as a queer person, I have been able to find a really strong and loving community that has supported me in my self-growth, and that has given me the chance to explore who I am as a person and become comfortable with it," Bri says. "And that wasn't something that I necessarily felt I could do everywhere."

Since coming to Yale, Bri has come out as both gay (to everyone, including their family) and gender-fluid.

And though Yale is far from the "perfect haven" Bri thought it would be, it has given them access to amazing opportunities, friends, and mentors, they explain. Bri advocates for better campus mental health resources through Project LETS "Eliminate the Stigma" and the elimination of the student income contribution with Students Unite Now, a community organization that advocates for lighter campus job requirements for students receiving financial aid. Through connections they made as a researcher at the School of Public Health and engaging with Yale fellowship funds, Bri spent ten weeks in Romania this summer conducting a research project about resilience among LGBT communities and individuals.

Now in their senior year of their undergraduate education, Bri serves as a first-year counselor in Pierson College. But they won't be leaving Yale too soon—Bri is a part of the five-year joint BA-BS/Master of Public Health program offered by Yale College and the Yale School of Public Health.

Bri's essays include one of their Yale supplemental essays.

ESSAY 1 (YALE SUPPLEMENT): IN THIS ESSAY, PLEASE REFLECT ON SOMETHING YOU WOULD LIKE US TO KNOW ABOUT YOU THAT WE MIGHT NOT LEARN FROM THE REST OF YOUR APPLICATION, OR ON SOMETHING ABOUT WHICH YOU WOULD LIKE TO SAY MORE. YOU MAY WRITE ABOUT ANYTHING—FROM PERSONAL EXPERIENCES OR INTERESTS TO INTELLECTUAL PURSUITS.

I stood up at the bottom of my High School's Greek Theater. I looked up to find 3,500 faces staring back down at me in silent expectation. The anticipation welled up in my stomach like an inner fire, fueled to become stronger with the air of each passing second.

The words began to stream out of my mouth. I couldn't really hear myself, but I had practiced it so many times that I didn't even need to. I then took a step back, and announced, "I am going to sing a parody of Lorde's Royals, which I call Vikings. The roar of applause pushed me forward.

I began to sing, but the fire of my nervousness was unrelenting, and a few lines in, I felt myself beginning to falter. It was then that something I never could have expected in my wildest dreams happened: the crowd began to sing along. "And we'll always be Vikings" I sang, and "Vikings" they echoed back to me. The crowd's energy kept me going, and I somehow made it to the end. "Let me be your ruler" I sang, and together their voices echoed "Ruler."

Three days later, students and teachers alike knew my name: I had won the ASB Presidency. It's crazy how things have turned out this way, how different my life has become. I can still recall my first day of elementary school.

"Hello, it's nice to meet you" I remember my teacher saying to me.

"*Shto?*" I responded. I had been suddenly launched into a school that functioned solely on English while only speaking Russian.

I was already a shy and quiet kid, so making friends would have been a leap out of my comfort zone that I wasn't ready to take. I stayed quiet, and instead found joy in books. Reading was an escape down the rabbit hole, an adventure, a solace, a fountain of wisdom. Unfortunately, learning and making friends were separate skill-sets. It was not until high school that I found my voice. I had to learn to be loud, be proud, and carry myself like I meant it.

After joining our Associated Student Body (ASB), I was constantly frustrated by the flaws in our school's leadership. When the time for election season came, I decided that I wanted to make a change, and chose to run for president.

I was the quieter candidate, the underdog, running against one of the most popular boys in school. From the start I knew that I had to give it my all. "We'll vote for you, but you do know that you probably won't win" was the response that I got from a majority of my friends. I knew that I had to prove them wrong, so I did. I campaigned to strangers and friends alike, and drew support from everyone I could. I finally came out of my comfort zone, and became the confident person I wanted to be.

Yannis Messaoui

Hometown: Paris, France

Year: Junior

College: Jonathan Edwards

Major(s): Economics

Extracurriculars: Senior Class President; Junior Class Council, vice president

PROFILE

You can say a lot about Paris, and you can say a lot about New Haven, but only one of the two cities has Yale. And for Yannis Messaoui—a Paris native, born and raised—Yale was enough.

Yannis says that he has always been exposed to "lots of English" moving through elite public schools in Paris and, for a short period of time, the Lycée Français de New York. This made the proposition of an American college experience feasible for Yannis, but neither an interest in English nor the desire to study abroad brought him across the Atlantic for his bachelor's degree. Rather, it was the lure of a liberal arts education and an opportunity to spend four years of college experimenting with a range of different academic interests that ultimately drew Yannis to Yale.

In France, Yannis complains, "everything is a ready-made path for you to follow." But whereas European colleges and even high schools tend to push students into specific career paths at early stages in their education, Yale allows—and even requires—undergraduates to study a broad range of academic topics before graduating, in the spirit of a liberal arts education. This held sway for Yannis.

"The name Yale drew me in from France in the first place," Yannis says. "I toured Yale in New Haven and absolutely loved Yale. We don't do the whole campus life back in Paris—and there's also so much freedom in Yale versus in France. I was looking for academic freedom."

Now a senior, Yannis has settled on a bachelor's degree in economics, but not before, he explains, trying out premed courses at Yale and experimenting with majors in global affairs, political science, and engineering.

In high school, Yannis experimented with a broad range of activities, from theater to model congress. At Yale, he says, not much has changed: He pursues a wide range of interests, including water polo, club swimming, Yale TV (YTV), and working at a student café. However, Yannis has been very devoted to student government at Yale. He has spent half of his time at Yale in class leadership and is committed as class secretary, the equivalent of senior class president. He will hold this position until 2024, planning reunions and alumni events until five years down the line.

According to Yannis, although he entered the university unsure of what he would enjoy most, his greatest joy at Yale has turned out to be engaging with his fellow students. One of his favorite memories from Yale was the Masquerade Ball, a formal dance that is held every spring to commemorate the Senior Class. "It was great to see all my friends together and having a great time. Plus," he adds jokingly, "my high school in France didn't have a prom."

"I thought I'd go in with an open mind but without any specific expectations. Especially freshman year, Yale was way better than what I thought it would be," Yannis says. "What I realized I loved most was just making connections with people . . . I have made so many friends at Yale, and I have learned so much."

His one misgiving about Yale? The students don't take the chance to visit New York enough, Yannis claims.

Yannis's essays include one of his Yale supplement essays.

ESSAY 1 (YALE SUPPLEMENT): PLEASE REFLECT ON SOMETHING YOU WOULD LIKE US TO KNOW ABOUT YOU THAT WE MIGHT NOT LEARN FROM THE REST OF YOUR APPLICATION, OR ON SOMETHING ABOUT WHICH YOU WOULD LIKE TO SAY MORE.

We feasted on empanadas and avocado, laughed to tears, and told stories of France and Chile. When I thanked the Ruz family for welcoming me in Santiago I felt blessed for speaking Spanish.

For as far as I can remember I have always wanted to learn Spanish. I started teaching myself when I was ten but it didn't pay off so I applied to the Spanish European Section in middle school unaware of what a life changing experience I was about to live.

Five hours a week my class met with Ms. Piotrowski, a dynamic blond woman knocking us out with Spanish grammar, vocabulary and culture. "Come on, *niños*, Spanish isn't a dead language! Breathe it, live it!" The first weeks were quite discouraging. Ms. Piotrowski was never satisfied; her expectations seemed out of reach. I didn't give up though, I clung to learning Spanish as hard as I could and, when I could eventually utter decent phrases and understand conversations, I realized that I could do whatever I wanted if I gave myself a shot.

Self-confidence was indeed the most important lesson the European Section taught me. My shyness vanished thanks to what Ms. Piotrowski called "the victims." She would randomly call out one name and have this student make a speech in Spanish in front of the whole class. My first "victimization" was horrendous but I strangely came to enjoy the exercise. I could be whatever I wanted to be, come up with new intonations and quirky retorts. When I was a victim I would lead the show and, gradually, the insecure boy I used to be before I entered the Section came out of his shell. I had discovered another facet of my personality: my love for acting. The Section turned out to be a wonderful opportunity to follow this passion. Every term, Ms. Piotrowski would divide the class into small groups that had to write and shoot a short video in Spanish. Not only did it develop my taste for teamwork, it allowed me to express my creativity though I may have acted less eccentrically had I known that my act disguised as a fortune-teller blithering in Spanish would be projected on a big screen in front of the whole class and the parents at the end-of-the-year party.

In the European Section I found a community where I belonged. A community cemented by team work and the same passion. I feel that the most gratifying point of this whole process was that it connected me to what makes us human. Learning a new language is a window onto different countries, cultures and individuals. I feel the diversity of the world we live in. I have built many great relationships thanks to this gift.

Learning Spanish helped me define my identity, it made me who I am. This experience turned me into a better person. I want to give this gift back and I hope college will provide me with the opportunity to do so.

Rachel Okun

Hometown: McLean, VA

Year: Junior

College: Timothy Dwight

Major(s): American Studies

Extracurriculars: Redhot&Blue
a cappella; writing partner

PROFILE

Rachel Okun is no stranger to ivory towers juxtaposed with cityscapes—the striking architecture of Yale College, which impresses many upon their arrival, did not faze Rachel one bit.

Rachel grew up in McLean, Virginia, a city outside Washington, D.C. According to Rachel, McLean is a place where people live but do not often stay. It is a commuter city, with many of its inhabitants traveling to and from the country's capital daily. In the spirit of the city, Rachel also commuted to her high school: the all-girls National Cathedral School. The close proximity of both Gothic architecture and a bustling city gave Rachel a unique high school experience. Because of this, Rachel described having "no culture shock" upon coming to Yale, "which was unsettling in and of itself," she said.

At Yale, Rachel joined the a cappella group Redhot&Blue—a group that initially focused on jazz repertoire but has since expanded to encompass other genres. Redhot&Blue was one of the first spaces in which Rachel felt a sense of "ecstatic belonging" at Yale. She described Redhot&Blue as the group in which she learned that "I could still be lovable even when I wasn't particularly lovely," and strong interpersonal connections were forged as a result.

Rachel's other extracurricular ventures at Yale were initiated through the Yale College Writing Center. She works as a writing partner and assists peers with their work through the Writing Center, and also takes part in the Sacred Texts and Social Justice program run by the Yale Divinity School—otherwise known as Dante Behind Bars. Dante Behind Bars allows students to lead weekly writing workshops based on Dante's *The Divine Comedy* in the MacDougall-Walker Correctional Institution.

Academically, Rachel is an American studies major who seeks to make a difference in educational systems. For her senior thesis, Rachel interviewed middle-school adolescents, questioning and probing the cliché that middle school is a universally unpleasant period of emotional development. These interests have led Rachel to consider doing work similar to that of the Yale Center for Emotional Intelligence, where academics seek to refine curriculum in a manner that emphasizes the critical role emotions play in teaching and learning.

Although Rachel is nearing the end of her time as an undergraduate at Yale, she does not fear losing the friendships she built. In her experience, the people she has encountered at Yale have been devoted to friendship to an extent that was surprising. For example, during Rachel's first year, one of her suitemates noticed the perennial smudges on Rachel's glasses. One day, Rachel came home to a packet of cleaning wipes taped to her door, accompanied by a message that said, "The world would be even brighter if your glasses were clean."

Rachel's essays include her Common App personal statement and three of her Yale supplemental essays.

ESSAY 1 (COMMON APP):
PERSONAL STATEMENT

TREASURING SERVICE

I have a treasure hunt for you.

Your goal: Find ThanksUSA, a 501(c)3 providing $3,000 scholarships to military dependents. My little sister and I birthed our brainchild eight years ago and, so far, ThanksUSA has awarded nearly $10 million in scholarships to over 3,000 children and spouses in all 50 states, across all military branches.

As your guide, I lend you my compass. The military became my true north when Lieutenant Colonel Lanier Ward and his family moved next door in 2005. The public's and my own attention was drifting away from the war effort in increments of neighborhood trees losing their yellow ribbons. Despite our patriotism, my community made Atlases of our military families, shrugging off our security concerns onto their shoulders. Two Purple Hearts in Iraq prevented Colonel Ward from carrying his daughter and, as I watched them walk to school hand-in-hand, I remember my heart aching the same way teeth do after eating ice cream too quickly. I wanted to thank the military with something more timeless than the tinsel that I stuffed into care packages. How do you repay someone who permits you to be the best version of yourself? I found my answer in the subliminal messages of my elementary school teachers: education is a conduit that allows dammed passion to flow forth and generate change. The gift of education could thank Colonel Ward on the front lines by empowering his family on the home front.

With your sense of direction established, you, like me, need a map from inspiration to positive action. Treasure hunts were a popular route after the film *National Treasure*, so my family, my third-grade teacher, and a kaleidoscope of characters gathered around the dinner table to design a virtual American history treasure hunt that inspired ThanksUSA's full name, Treasure Hunt Aiding the Needs of Kids and Spouses of those serving the United States of America, and encouraged donations for scholarships.

You have arrived! When you unearth ThanksUSA, you will find a hoard of multifaceted gems. In one facet, anecdotes from recipients, from first-generation students to spouses returning to college, have illustrated college's incalculable worth. Academics promote thoughtful questions and incisive analysis, student diversity presents a range of role models, and an unrivaled safety net inclines lifelong learners to leaps of faith. On another plane, I can see my future in education reform, based on a belief that schools should offer mobility contingent on merit and work ethic, the essence of the American Dream our military preserves. On yet another plane, ThanksUSA has linked what I believe in my heart with what I believe I can do, a connection that I hope to share with my classmates as my school's current Service Board President.

During my tenure, I have endeavored to help each girl discover a compass and map to facilitate her own treasure hunt. Service trips put the "compass" in compassion by introducing girls to a variety of "poles," magnetically attractive causes that, like ThanksUSA, might induce lifelong purpose. Recently, I considered a map of my school's culture and decided we could channel the fandom surrounding the dystopian book/movie series, *The Hunger Games,* toward something noble by initiating "The (End) Hunger Games," a five-school fundraiser styled as Assassin, where the victor will donate the schools' joint jackpot to a local charity. While ThankUSA's compass-and-map model guides my short-term goals, digging into ThanksUSA's treasure trove reveals my long-term goal. The military epitomizes a mindset that I hope my peers and I can adopt: service is a mentality, a way of life rather than a day in life. This philosophy could refashion the NCS acronym so that it represents not just National Cathedral School, but a new mantra: Never Cease Serving. As I serve, I search for myself, but my X-marks-the-spot never changes: my heart is in my (treasure) chest. In looking for ThanksUSA, you have found me.

ESSAY 2 (YALE SUPPLEMENT): WHAT IN PARTICULAR ABOUT YALE HAS INFLUENCED YOUR DECISION TO APPLY?

The musical *That's Why I Chose Yale* added a deal breaker to my criteria: students happy enough to break into song. On my tour, I was thrilled to find that joy of learning embodied by both Yalies and their "Cathedral to Knowledge." Loquacious tour guide Sanjena Sathian spoke volumes, through word and example, about how Yale encourages both applicants and accepted students to be their best selves. I love this quintessential Yale attitude and the extent to which it permeates the Y* Apply website: Yale is the only college on my list that links advice portals to its writing supplement.

ESSAY 3 (YALE SUPPLEMENT): SHORT TAKES

You have been granted a free weekend next month. How will you spend it?

10:45 am: Bolt Bus arrives in New York City. 12–3 pm: Master class with Tony-Award winner Laura Benanti. 4–7 pm: Listen to Guest Choir at St. Patrick's.

What is something about which you have changed your mind in the last three years?

I should learn for myself rather than my mentors, for the sake of ingesting rather than impressing.

What is the best piece of advice you have received while in high school?

I asked my brilliant physics professor, "How can I become as smart as you are?" "Read. Read what intrigues you and you won't forget it."

What do you wish you were better at being or doing?

Telling funny stories. In a figurative family variety show, my sister and I write the jokes together, but she's the comedian and I'm the laugh track.

What is a learning experience, in or out of the classroom, that has had a significant impact on you?

My current English teacher provides critiques in the form of questions, proving that criticism can push a person forward as opposed to down.

ESSAY 4 (YALE SUPPLEMENT): IN THIS ESSAY, PLEASE REFLECT ON SOMETHING YOU WOULD LIKE US TO KNOW ABOUT YOU THAT WE MIGHT NOT LEARN FROM THE REST OF YOUR APPLICATION, OR ON SOMETHING ABOUT WHICH YOU WOULD LIKE TO SAY MORE.

I have never seen the "fun" in perfunctory. I gravitate toward the magnum opus rather than the minimum effort, one of many tropisms I attribute to the environment of competitive horseback riding. As input seldom equals output in a sport involving animals instead of inanimate objects, you learn to give your best merely because offering your partner anything less is sacrilege. My horse's simplest gestures humble me. When I rub Annie's neck, I mimic the motion of predators searching for her jugular vein, yet she fights her flight instincts. While Annie chooses to throw off years of evolutionary history instead of me, I embrace another adaptation from my equestrian past: blinders for benchmarks. The word "riding" evokes open spaces and long roads and the discipline itself emphasizes the journey. Focusing on the process—be it the alignment of Annie's spine while approaching a jump or my cognitive cogs turning during a test—reduces literal and figurative obstacles to speed bumps that simply offer feedback on my progress.

While barn soil has nurtured me for eleven years, my roots are loosening because I know that I cannot replicate my relationship with Annie without Virginia dirt and because my continued growth depends upon uprooting. Recently, after a customarily frantic costume change in the car from (horse) show clothes to (choir) show clothes, I cantered into rehearsal with muddy pastures beneath my fingernails and the impression of my helmet still stamped across my forehead. The tang of fly spray leavened the scent of hay and my trainer's chain-smoke, and as both the smells and Brahms's Requiem dissipated throughout the National Cathedral, I mused that I should be more like the Cathedral acoustics, clarifying, beautifying, and amplifying the ideas incident upon me in class discussion. Suddenly, from the vantage point of the risers, riding looked like a science experiment that only exposed me, the subject, to a set of controlled stimuli. However, if I want to flourish, I need new influences to catalyze revelations like this one and to coax out dormant traits. If I am lucky enough to choose my new environment, I hope to be replanted at Yale.

Yale's rich loam is replete with courses like Directed Studies, a singular opportunity to sink roots into the bedrock texts of Western civilization and prune my analytical skills. Sixty-one performing arts groups can plant new seeds in the hole that riding leaves. While coverage of current Rhodes scholars provides a drip-feed of inspiration, the Residential Colleges will plant me alongside one-of-a-kind sprouts and the Master's Teas will introduce me to the mentors who cultivate *Yaleus discipulus*. This species is my favorite because it itches to extend itself, like the ivy sprawling across the campus's Gothic architecture. However, this breed's defining characteristic is photosynthesis, its ability to reemit what it absorbs in a manner benefiting the entire greenhouse. Without riding, I will be laden with a surplus of passion that I can use to return the favor and replenish the soil.

Kendrick Umstattd

Hometown: Leesburg, VA

Year: Junior

College: Benjamin Franklin

Major(s): Electrical Engineering & Computer Science

Extracurriculars: Society of Women Engineers; *Yale Scientific Magazine,* writer; Yale Resonance Conference

PROFILE

While Kendrick Umstattd was thinking of where to apply to college, an alum from her high school who attended Yale came to give a talk about her time at the university. The alum brought along a copy of *Yale Scientific Magazine*. After attending the meeting—and reading the magazine—Kendrick knew that she wanted to apply to Yale. Once Kendrick was accepted, the admissions office set up a phone call between her and a current Yale student also interested in robotics and computer science. The conversation convinced Kendrick that Yale was the right choice for her.

Now, at Yale, the Virginia native is an electrical engineering and computer science double major. In addition to her work with the Yale Robotics Lab and tenure as the Webmaster for Benjamin Franklin College, Kendrick is a member of Yale's Society of Women Engineers and a writer for *Yale Scientific Magazine*. Kendrick says that before college, she had been focused on finding a cause to serve that was bigger than herself, and she spent her high school years leading a community service club and cofounding a robotics club. Kendrick was eager to pursue these passions after meeting classmates who were similarly motivated.

Over the past three years, Kendrick has participated in the Yale Resonance Conference, an annual conference seeking to inspire high schoolers to pursue science through seminars and science-related activities and lab tours, as a speaker, a teacher, and as a director. Beyond Yale, she has brought her passion for encouraging more young women to pursue computer science and engineering to her internships at Google, where she will work full-time as a software engineer upon graduation. She organized and held a Made with Code coding event for local teen girls to empower them to pursue computer science, and also served as the first intern team member of the Women of Silicon Valley and produced the 2018 Intern Series to highlight female interns through Medium articles and social media posts.

During Kendrick's first year at Yale, a member of the Yale Social Robotics Lab gave a lecture in her Introduction to Cognitive Science class. Inspired by the talk, Kendrick joined the lab and worked on a project creating socially assistive robots that could help teach autistic children social skills. They deployed the robots in households across the United States in early 2018.

Kendrick says she cannot choose just one favorite memory of Yale, but her top three are Yale's famous first-year holiday dinner—hosted in the massive Commons dining hall—and its "Hogwarts energy"; creating traditions in Benjamin Franklin after its founding in 2017; and, finally, greeting dining hall staff at meals because it "feels like seeing family." Kendrick says that there is not one specific experience that makes Yale so important to her; rather, it is the holistic sense of a welcoming, loving community that makes Yale feel like home.

Kendrick's essays include her Common App personal statement.

ESSAY 1 (COMMON APP):
PERSONAL STATEMENT
Reflect on a time when you challenged a belief or idea. What prompted you to act? Would you make the same decision again?

I grew up with activist parents in a rapidly diversifying town. My mother was the mayor and my father was a lawyer who worked pro bono for disadvantaged clients. I had seen the value of giving a voice to those who might otherwise be ignored. I didn't know, however, that high school would give me a chance to do so.

With over a hundred members, Keyettes is my high school's largest service club. As a freshman, I joined because I knew that my capacity to help the community would be amplified by working with a varied, talented group. I had previously raised hundreds of dollars for St. Jude's Children's Hospital with my Tae-Kwon-Do dojang, and I felt the same energy from the Keyettes that I had felt from my martial arts fundraising team.

At the Keyettes' initial meetings, the freshmen and sophomores chatted excitedly before the senior officers spoke, discussing the upcoming events in which they wanted to participate. We wanted to be involved and to help those who were less fortunate. But I watched some of this excitement leave the faces of the underclassmen, including mine, when the seniors gave the underclassmen little opportunity to participate. I was disheartened that the message we heard was that the club was for the upperclassmen. Hoping to change this, even though, as I was told later, it was against club rules, I ran for officer at the end of my freshman year, becoming the first sophomore to be voted in as an officer of the club.

At first, I believed that my election would end the two-tiered system. I worked closely with the younger members, listening to their ideas and trying to relay them to the seniors with whom I was working. The other officers, however, had a different idea, and that idea did not include giving underclassmen a chance to shape the club or our interaction with the community. "Seniors Only" service activities were created, and the club's ability to serve the public was diminished.

I was able to work around the senior officers to an extent, and I coordinated the 2013 annual fashion show to raise money for the Cystic Fibrosis Foundation. I ensured that the underclassmen were involved in every aspect of preparation: baking for the bake sale, modeling, and decorating. As underclassmen worked to prepare, I saw the club's potential increase, and, more importantly, I saw how happy the members were to be given the opportunity to contribute. I wanted to preserve this excitement, so, with permission from the club's faculty sponsor, I ran for Keyettes president, despite the senior officers' protests that only rising seniors could run.

Reaching out to underclassmen, I won on the platform that I would protect their voice in the club.

As president of Keyettes my junior year, I safeguarded the ideas of those who had been marginalized. For the first time, all members voted on activities that they wanted. The senior officers, with whom I served, wanted to cancel the 2014 fashion show, taking away the club's best opportunity to raise money— this time for Backpack Buddies, a group which provides food to our underprivileged students. I notified all members, urging them to attend the next meeting and show their support for the fundraiser. Many underclassmen came and voted in favor of the show. On the day of the event, I watched as a record number of underclassmen showed up to prepare.

At the end of my presidency, I focused on the fact that the

leadership was all white and, except for me, all seniors. The officers weren't fully representative of those who wanted to serve the club and the community. I encouraged freshmen, sophomores and minority students to run for office. The officers are no longer exclusively white, and there are now two underclassmen who serve. I am proud that this small step forward for inclusion is my contribution to my school.

Neche Veyssal

Hometown: Milwaukee, WI

Year: Junior

College: Berkeley

Major(s): Applied Mathematics

Extracurriculars: Berkeley College
Orchestra; QuestBridge chapter

PROFILE

Neche is a junior in Berkeley College majoring in applied mathematics. Her favorite book is *Firegirl* by Tony Abbott, she listens to a lot of EDM music, and she's never seen the end of a movie because she always falls asleep in the middle.

In high school, Neche was the smart girl who played the viola. While she considered double majoring in math and music, she ultimately decided to major only in math. She liked her math classes better than her music classes, and even when she was taking non-math classes, she found herself thinking about the science behind them, so she decided to pursue her interests in STEM.

Neche's favorite classes include Data Analysis, Turkish, and a first-year seminar called Literature, Media, and Weather. In fact, meteorology is one of her biggest interests, and she is considering attending graduate school to study the climate sciences.

Outside the classroom, Neche plays the viola in the Berkeley College Orchestra and numerous pit orchestras. She loves that, through music, she can express herself without words. Her favorite piece is *Fantasie* by Johann Hummel.

Other than playing the viola, Neche is also a member of Yale's QuestBridge Chapter—she's an expert at explaining to others what it's like to be a first-generation, low-income college student. She has helped start an organization named FGLI (First-Generation/Low-Income Students at Yale) to further these efforts.

In addition, Neche is a member of the Yale Bulgarian Society. Her goals at Yale include learning Turkish and Bulgarian, her ancestral language, in order to be able to better communicate with her family members. She has achieved the former, and is in the process of achieving the latter.

Neche likes to explore New Haven; she enjoys taking the bus and discovering new streets, having conversations with locals, and people-watching. Her favorite spot in the city is the Ella B. Scantlebury Playground, located just north of campus.

Neche also likes to spend time with her friends. Together, they go to different restaurants, dance at parties, hang out in each other's suites talking for hours, go for nighttime walks, and sit on the swing, looking up at the sky.

And her favorite thing about Yale? Feeling like she belongs there, being able to find a really close group of friends, having a sense of support and community, and knowing that everyone wants her to have a good college experience.

Neche's essays include her Common App personal statement.

ESSAY 1 (COMMON APP):
PERSONAL STATEMENT

Waiting at the mailbox. Waiting at the library inside whatever school I am at that day. Waiting for the first rehearsal to begin. All of these places have one thing in common, which is they all show what improvements I have made in performing on my lovely Annabelle and now Victor, my viola.

I have a fear of performing in front of people, whether it be on giving a class presentation to competing for a solo at a concert. Actually, scratch that—I have a fear of disappointing people. From this, I get nervous when it comes to presenting anything in front of people. I didn't grow up with the typical large family; I grew up with my parents, brother, and a computer providing a portal to where I had apparently immigrated from and where my large family lived. My parents came with my four-month-old self to the United States with our visas and a distant relative's apartment to live at. I grew up with one foreign friend and my small family, so showing off my talents to others wasn't a strong suit.

My strong suit was (and still is) learning/teaching. I taught a couple of cousins how to speak English to help rid the language barrier a little bit, and I was learning every spare moment I had, since there were no luxuries of expensive toys or family vacations. In elementary school, I was focused on the weather and medicine. I strived to learn so that I could provide my family with the luxuries they deserved, and to prove my dad wrong in his sayings of our futures were gas store clerks/ grocery store baggers. That all changed in sixth grade, though, when I had finally convinced my mom to let me learn an instrument: the viola.

She was convinced it was going to be like everything else; I'd be interested for a couple of weeks and then ditch it from fear. She was wrong; seven years later the viola is still going strong and has grown to be a key characteristic of my life. It used to be just a class and something I could show to my distant family without the need to translation to understand. However, in eighth grade my teacher suggested I go audition for the Milwaukee Youth Symphony Orchestra (MYSO). I thought it was a long stretch; there was no way that after three years I'd be good enough to get into the program, but I agreed to try anyways. She gave me a couple of lessons to prepare, and said that I should be able to get into Sinfonia, the third-highest string group overall (at the time) and the highest string-only group. I remember entering the warm-up room, following all of the advice given before, and praying I wouldn't disappoint. I completed my audition, thought I did alright, and waited in agony the next two months for the letter determining my fate.

Finally, it arrived, and with my palms sweaty with excitement, I open the letter and bam. Not only had I gotten in, but I had gotten into Philharmonia, the second-highest group and one of two symphony orchestras (at the time). Everyone was blown away, and has been with every audition/performance since. While it took a while to start getting over my fear, I had managed to be a part of Wisconsin State Honors Orchestra twice, attend state solo/ensemble every year in multiple events with good scores resulting, and recently go with MYSO's Senior Symphony (highest group) to a tour in Europe with four sold-out concerts.

Through music, I had achieved the reason that my parents moved to the United States: to build a better future and provide endless opportunities. I hope to continue on with music education and math in college to be able to teach students in fundamental skills both intellectually and artistically.

Yvonne Ye

Hometown: Saratoga, CA

Year: Junior

College: Berkeley

Major(s): East Asian Languages & Literatures

Extracurriculars: A Different Drum Dance Company; Groove Dance Company; Club Ultimate Frisbee; Yale College Writing Center, writing partner

PROFILE

Yvonne Ye graduated from high school in Shanghai and lived there for three years, so on most official records, she's an international student because she applied from abroad. "Originally," however, she says she is from California. Yvonne's hesitations about what her hometown is mirror the conflicting linguistic and cultural choices within her essay, between the city she grew up in and the city that is home to her parents. She writes, "No amount of steamed buns could fill that hole in my soul where my hometown used to be."

As a college student, however, Yvonne has found that she has had greater opportunities to really understand who she is and where she belongs in "a changing, modernizing world." As she answers the hometown question, she muses to herself about the evolution of her identity. She thinks college has opened up avenues for expression through conversation and discourse that she did not have access to in high school;

earlier, she did not have the vocabulary to express what she was thinking or feeling.

"High School Me was a lot less sure about things. High School Me is very much like College Me—but without all the rough edges sanded off."

Yvonne's personal evolution and openness to change is a parallel to her openness in exploring her interests. She says she was never a theater person. She always said in high school that she would *never* do theater.

"Guess what I'm involved in now?" She giggles.

As Yvonne speaks and gesticulates in equal parts to explain her answers, she often erupts in quick bouts of laughter between sentences. She tells me the main reason why she chose Yale was that she had heard people say that Yale students were happy.

"When I came to college, I was like, 'This is what happiness is.'"

This contentment is not, however, isolated to Yvonne's experience at Yale. She presumes, with unquestioning optimism, that she will keep discovering that her happiness increases at each stage of her life.

Yvonne thought deeply about her favorite memory at Yale, arriving at an answer after a few minutes of sifting between many contenders. During first-year orientation, she was walking along the path between Berkeley College, Trumbull College, and Sterling Memorial Library. As she was walking around, she looked at all the Gothic buildings, the leaves starting to turn, the Harkness bells ringing.

"I remember looking around and being like—I hope I never get used to this. Now I am used to it, but every time I think of that I'm like—*yeah.*" She exhales and smiles.

Yvonne's essays include her Common App personal statement and one of her Yale supplemental essays.

ESSAY 1 (COMMON APP):
PERSONAL STATEMENT
Some students have a background or story so central to their identity that they believe their application would be incomplete without it. Share this story.

SHANGHAI
I have a curious choice to make every time I pronounce this city's name, like deciding between two sides of a conflict: Do I speak in the tongue of the town I was born in or in the language of the land I live in?

"*SHANG*-hai." I come as a foreigner, accenting the first syllable, twisting the *A* into the curve of my lips as the word twangs in my mouth. Born and bred in Californian sunshine, I hated this city of haze at first with a simmering fire in my gut that clawed its way into notebooks full of acrid words. A prisoner of my father's job, I discovered in the next six months that no amount of steamed buns could fill that hole in my soul where my hometown used to be. I burned my first bridges in that flight across the Pacific; left drifting, I struggled to learn how to pronounce the slang of the city like a local, to acclimatize my tongue to the new way names rolled from my lips.

"Shang*HA-AI*." But sometimes I defend the besieged stronghold, my adopted city, opening up the soft palate so "ah" comes out in the first syllable before bouncing through the second one. Accents make all the difference in local supermarkets here, where the slightest slip-up in your vowels can expose you as nonnative. But now, that fear doesn't stop me from chatting with taxi drivers on my way to dance practice anymore; every person I can convince that I'm not foreign-born is a small victory in the uphill battle of learning the language of my parents.

Adjusting to life in China requires more than a tectonic shift of mindset; reality lies in a long war of attrition—a personal ten-year siege of Troy. I did not embrace Shanghai all at once; slowly, haltingly, I accepted truces. Late night strolls weren't so bad, I admitted, and the new people—friends from Canada, Denmark, New Jersey, and even the sandwich deli lady—were as fascinating and compelling as any Greek or Trojan hero. Through conversations as short as ordering a vegetarian panini or as long as shared plane flights to a forensics competition, they helped me realize that unhappiness has always been a choice. I needed to reassess the values that directed my life, to look around with wonder instead of prejudice. Because even after the war ended and Troy fell, it was rebuilt; and even as I fought air pollution and reckless drivers, idiomatic grammar and my own biases, Shanghai reforged me with the defiance of its people and the steel of its skyscrapers. Wars don't make people; wars *change* people.

Two years later, I smile at the shopkeepers I once feared, switching languages as easily as jackets. I make small talk with security guards and savor the rare days of pollution-free air. Now I see the fortune I have to live in an international forum, filled with snapshots of lives across cultures and continents—a place where we can learn from each other even as we laugh, where we sing the cadences of our sentences that pay homage to our countries of origin.

"I live in—Shanghai." I still wobble between accents, stumbling before the word as I remember where I am. "But I'm originally from California." Sometimes, my American tongue wins out; others, Chinese rolls from my lips with rich authenticity. Language used to mark the front where my cultures clashed with each other. Now, it opens new paths that lead me off into undiscovered regions, familiar and exotic. This internal war has given me open palms and words in three languages, grounded me in knowing who I am and what I love, and made me ready to adapt to and appreciate the world, wherever the winds blow me.

ESSAY 2 (YALE SUPPLEMENT): PLEASE REFLECT ON SOMETHING YOU WOULD LIKE US TO KNOW ABOUT YOU THAT WE MIGHT NOT LEARN FROM THE REST OF YOUR APPLICATION, OR ON SOMETHING ABOUT WHICH YOU WOULD LIKE TO SAY MORE. YOU MAY WRITE ABOUT ANYTHING— FROM PERSONAL EXPERIENCES OR INTERESTS TO INTELLECTUAL PURSUITS.

Would you look at that, I thought, staring down at the paper. *Plan B actually worked.*

I held the very first copy of *Confection: A Literary Magazine* in my hands, its black-and-white pages still warm from the printer. Handling each sheet gingerly, I scanned the familiar spreads. There was Aaron, grinning cheekily from his double page. Below, Tiffany's artwork spidered across the margins in graceful lines. I knew each photo, each page, each pica. I had fought with the formatting and font sizes and laid out all the columns and captions, stealing minutes between classes and hours from my sleep to tweak the designs and rearrange the poems yet again. Thirty-two pages slowly emerged from the art and writing that my fellow high schoolers had submitted.

"You can keep the advance copy," the lady who ran the print center said kindly, and I stammered out a thanks.

Here is a confession: I'd never run a magazine before.

Here is another confession: I made it up as I went along.

When the original editor-in-chief unexpectedly abdicated, the literary magazine club fell into my inexperienced hands. I was just beginning my second year at a new school overseas and trying to handle a club that had held only two meetings last year—once to meet each other, and once for the yearbook photo.

That wouldn't cut it this year, I decided. Writing outside of class wasn't especially popular among kids who often spoke a different language at home. I wanted to give them the opportunity to see their work in print to spur their continued interest.

There was a slight problem in this otherwise bulletproof plan: no one else in the club knew the mechanics of making a magazine, and not many had the time to learn how to wrangle the layout software into obedience. During first semester, publication stalled as I tried to teach club members about pica blocks while coaxing them to write in their free time.

Once second semester hit the ground, however, the deadline for getting printed loomed ominously close. There simply wasn't enough *time* for everyone to reach the fluency in InDesign needed to lay out their own pages before exam season.

Thus, plan B came into play—with a single-minded intensity and my typical bulldog tenacity, I threw myself into laying out the entire magazine on my own. Club members contributed material; I wrestled the poems into place, matchmade artwork with fiction, and even found a company willing to defray the printing costs in exchange for advertising. In less than a month, the pages grew into the literary magazine that I now held in my hands.

As I headed toward the high school, a slow grin overtook my face. This was a publication made by high schoolers, and high schoolers alone—not a single teacher had a hand in it.

Aaron waved to me from the bleachers. I waved back, holding up the copy of *Confection*. "Litmag's out," I called triumphantly.

Seniors

Edgar Aviña

Hometown: Houston, TX

Year: Senior

College: Benjamin Franklin

Major(s): Political Science

Extracurriculars: La Unidad Latina service fraternity; Public School Internship Program

PROFILE

When Edgar Aviña first arrived at Yale, he had an unconventional goal for his next four years. Edgar's interest in architecture and urban planning drew him to Yale's campus as a senior in high school, and as a student he was determined to live in a different building each year. He later achieved that goal, living in Vanderbilt Hall as a first-year and then Saybrook, Silliman and, finally, Benjamin Franklin. (Only about 1 percent of Yale students transfer to a new residential college each year.)

Edgar's love for architecture developed in his hometown of Houston, Texas, where he grew up cycling across the city. The son of two immigrants from Mexico, Edgar worked odd jobs as a teenager to help support his family financially. At ten years old, he started his own lawn-mowing business, using his "cute little looks" to appeal to customers. Though he eventually outgrew his boyish charm, Edgar loved cutting grass and continued doing it until he left for college.

At Yale, Edgar majored in political science and participated in the Education Studies Scholars program. "I found Texas interesting as a political case study. I grew up in a Mexican barrio surrounded by Mexicans and a lot of people who were really progressive. Why is this state that's 40 percent Latino voting so drastically different compared to California, which is also roughly 40 percent Latino?" Edgar says. "I think that contrast, that contradiction, drew me to political science."

Edgar's college experience at Yale was defined by his involvement in two student groups: his service fraternity La Unidad Latina and the Public School Internship Program. With other fraternity members, Edgar was able to discuss his upbringing and the culture of machismo, which he says was "really productive for me in terms of learning how to become a better man and a better human being in general." Edgar adds that his internship, which placed him in a local elementary school for two years, helped confirm his desire to become an educator.

Upon graduation, Edgar will work as an eighth-grade science teacher in his hometown. Edgar's own eighth-grade teacher helped change the trajectory of his life, he says, by pushing him to apply to a top-tier high school. Without her intervention, he "may have not gone to college, much less Yale University." Now, as an educator himself, he hopes to inspire his own students—most of whom live under the poverty line—to dream big.

Edgar's essays include his Common App personal statement and one of his Yale supplemental essays.

ESSAY 1 (COMMON APP):
PERSONAL STATEMENT

CUTTING
Rivers of sweat snake around my body, soaking my ragged belt, drenching my grass-encrusted shirt, simmering as they channel

into the scalding blacktop road that slowly fries my feet. My fingers loop themselves around the string and tug. The gas trimmer coughs and gurgles to life with a black outburst of grime.

I cut. I cut away at the lumps of unruly vegetation. I cut a circle of lawn around the mailbox post. I cut, ignoring my parched throat, which begs for hydration. I cut away at my uneasiness, forgetting in this moment of toil my father's state of health. I cut, trying to dig my mother out of a mound of hospital bills.

I trudge home for two miles, dragging the lawnmower in one hand as my stiff arm desperately clutches the weed-eater with the other. My mother sits on the trailer steps, blank, listless, unreadable. I reach into my pocket, hand her the wad of crumpled bills, and stagger to the sofa, falling into a deep sleep.

The next day, I stride into my high school and flash my typical smile, crooked teeth and all. For now, nothing is wrong with me; I'm back in my oasis of comfort. I cheerfully go through the motions of a regular school day: wolfing down factory-manufactured cafeteria food, spending lunch in the library to bury my nose into a random volume of the *World Book Encyclopedia*, chuckling at my teacher's chemistry jokes.

I am two-faced. At home, I speak Spanish, wear a face of exhaustion, work with my coarse hands, cut grass, and refuse to speak from fear, fear of what will befall my father, who is in the Neurological ICU. At school, I communicate in English, manifest my happiness with a constant grin, work with my sharpened brain, cut incisively into the meaning of various books, and ramble about hyperbolas, the Houston Rockets, and Hemingway to distance myself from my reality at home.

Honestly, it is rather difficult to juggle my family world—where nobody is educated, where books are seen as good firewood, not mental stimulation, where my hands, not my mind, are my most powerful tool, where I cut up pancakes with my grubby fingers—with my school world, where everybody is expected to think critically, to read, to learn, to be sophisticated and cultured, where people cut up their pancakes with the fine, precise maneuverings of a knife and fork. However, I continue to inject optimism into my life. The school, my last bastion of contentment, wonder and carefree inquiry, is still there to embrace me with its culture of curiosity.

Countless manicured lawns, sparkling cars, and various odd jobs later, rays of hope emerge. My father has pulled out of his coma. He stammers out one word: "agua." He cups his hands and pleads for it. The apple doesn't fall far from the tree, does it? Water, the thought that tortures my mind most as the sun bakes me while I cut grass . . . water, what unites father and son.

Finally at home, my father sits in his chair, the one that wobbles and has Spider-Man and Pokémon stickers plastered on it. I lay sprawled out on the plastic tile kitchen floor. As always, we do not talk much. He leads through example, not the opening and closing of his mouth. My father simply stares at me. I simply stare back.

He waggles his thick finger. I report to his side immediately; he places a cold metal object in my palm. It's a two-peso coin, the same coin his own father had given to him before he set off for the U.S. from Mexico at the age of sixteen. No words need to be exchanged; the message is clear. I have fended for my family, working outside endlessly, cutting through the thickets of life's hardships. In the eyes of my father, I am now a man.

ESSAY 2 (YALE SUPPLEMENT): PLEASE REFLECT ON SOMETHING YOU WOULD LIKE US TO KNOW ABOUT YOU THAT WE MIGHT NOT LEARN FROM THE REST OF YOUR APPLICATION, OR ON SOMETHING ABOUT WHICH YOU WOULD LIKE TO SAY MORE.

The first time I explored Houston on my own, my butt flattened, my arms and face were burned into globs of pink, purple, and painful tenderness by the sun, and my legs were immobilized. I set out on my bike in August 2009 with a specific plan: to pedal aimlessly around Houston. I filled a jug with ice and tap water, placed it in my backpack, and churned away, on my way to unintentionally biking fifty-five miles.

My motivation was not exercise, but curiosity. I set out to discover the usually unnoticed details in the streets and structures, to *feel* the throbbing pulse of the city. As I began to pedal, I was drawn into a world of wonder. My eyebrows went up, and I could not get them to come back down again!

The city mirrored my passions. Williams Tower, enveloped by webs of sparkling blue glass, resembled the sheer complexity of the blue clock of Yale's Harkness Tower. The endless mazes of warehouses and oil refineries in the East End reminded me of my blue collar background. The Beer Can House in Montrose fed my never-ending hunger and near-obsession with public art. The seas of domino-like bookshelves in the Jesse H. Jones Library took me back to my childhood, when I would sneak into the library's third-floor private conference rooms to admire the pictures in the architecture books and slowly trace the outlines of the many buildings with my stubby index finger.

The route maps on the Metro bus stops wrenched me from my bike with the force of their simple beauty; my eyes carefully inspected the loops, twists, and turns of the labyrinthine street grid—just as they had done with countless other maps of Harris County and Houston. The mural on the Fiesta supermarket near Airline Drive, which depicted a Mexican family, reminded me of the innumerable piñatas, bowls of spicy salsa, rooster-like ranchero singing, *tapatio* hat dances, and the backbreaking yet fortifying construction work I had enjoyed over the years.

Houston's public transportation leaves something to be desired. My bike rides have convinced me that the city needs a better mass transit system. After all, the freeways aren't going to expand forever. The invigorating bike rides have cemented my decision: I want to become an urban planner. I want to be involved in laying out streets, in fomenting the creation of sustainable buildings, and, more than anything, in making efficient public transportation a reality in Houston.

Yale would be a perfect laboratory. I would have easy access to a phenomenal mass transit system: the MTA Metro-North Railroad. New Haven, snuggled between Boston and New York City, would be a perfect launching pad; from there, I would be able to go explore the trains of multiple cities. I want to investigate how in the world the Northeast has built up such an impressive rail-based mass transit system! My bike and I are ready to hop on New Haven's MTA train and find out.

Elijah Gunther

Hometown: Cambridge, MA

Year: Senior

College: Branford

Major(s): Mathematics (intensive)

Extracurriculars: Danceworks; Bad Romantics of Yale

PROFILE

As a high schooler, Elijah Gunther was the type of kid who loved math so much he quite literally dreamed about it. But math was not enough to take up all of Elijah's time during the day.

Elijah spent much of his time on sports—namely sailing, soccer and gymnastics—along with pursuits in the arts that included drawing, painting, and dancing in his school's modern dance company. Once the dust of college admissions had settled, Elijah had a choice between Yale or Harvard, and he chose to venture beyond his Cambridge roots.

As a Yale student, Elijah has not skipped a beat in following his passions and interests, no matter how disconnected they might seem. Throughout his time at Yale, Elijah completed a degree in mathematics, on an intensive track, while performing for Yale's Danceworks troupe, participating in drag shows with the Bad Romantics of Yale, and reciting poetry with the Voke Spoken Word group, all while finding time to toss Frisbees with the Yale's men's Ultimate Frisbee team, Süperfly.

Although Elijah came to Yale with few expectations, he did hope to become part of a strong community, and he presumed to find that community in his residential college. But this did not turn out to be the case. Instead, Elijah forged his strongest community bonds with friends he made through extracurriculars and math classes.

These communities became some of his favorite pieces of his Yale experience. Many of his favorite places—like the Davenport College buttery, where his Frisbee team held regular team dinners—and his favorite traditions at Yale, such as the rituals and team-bonding on Süperfly spring break trips, centered around his experiences with his Frisbee teammates and the connections they'd formed with each other.

Aside from the great groups of people he found over his time in college, Elijah said one of the things he really likes about Yale were the customs and events that were "memorable and specific to Yale," such as naked parties and their social dynamics.

"I remember going to [a naked party], and only one other friend was there, so I mainly chatted with him. I guess I didn't have much to say, so I was talking about topology with him," Elijah says. "Where other than Yale would I be standing around naked—in a room full of naked people—talking about topology?"

Now that his time at Yale has come to an end, Elijah will spend five years studying mathematics—which he still finds "just as fun and as cool and as magical" to study as when he first began rigorously studying mathematics in high school—in a doctorate program at the University of Pennsylvania.

Elijah's essays include his Common App personal statement and three of his Yale supplemental essays.

ESSAY 1 (COMMON APP):
PERSONAL STATEMENT

I carefully pull myself up between the pressure-treated joists and step onto the red oak floor. Encompassing me are verdant leaves sparkling in the sun. At this height, I see nothing but trees and my friends' smiling faces. Gradually, the wind begins to stir the treetops. Their rustling accompanies the ever-present song of the brook far below. Although the forest surrounding me shimmers with the wind, I feel perfectly secure. I trust that the floor of this incipient treehouse can easily bear our weight.

Since childhood, I have always been making things: first Thomas the Tank Engine railways and watercolors on paper, then working my way up to Rube Goldberg machines, Lego clocks, and oils on canvas. I engage myself in creation, always aspiring to increasingly challenging projects. When my family bought land in the mountains of New Hampshire a few years ago, I saw it as the perfect opportunity to build a treehouse.

I began by scouting potential sites. Over the course of months, I trekked across acres of forest, carefully weighing the pros and cons of numerous locations. Finally, with the guidance of my father, I picked a set of four trees upon which to build the treehouse.

The planning alone would have made the whole project worthwhile. On many wonderful nights my father and I stayed up late, exchanging visions and sketches, slowly settling on a design. I love chatting with my father into the early morning about something we both enjoy. There's nothing better than our minds churning together and producing incredible ideas.

The actual building of the treehouse was fun in a very different way. Whereas designing is cerebral, building is physical. It allows me to see my once-abstract plans come to fruition. Although my mind's eye can imagine any sort of fantastical treehouse, it is what I see before me that provides a sense of accomplishment. While designing provides the pleasure of intellectual collaboration, I also relish the camaraderie which comes from the experience of shared physical labor. It is exhilarating to stand upon the structure which I built with my own two hands and erected with the help of my friends and family.

From the start, I had wanted a treehouse which would give me a sense of seclusion. I wanted to feel like I was floating, ten feet up, in the middle of the woods. I wanted to be like Emerson's transparent eyeball, such that I could look all around and admire the trees, take in the tranquility. Consequently, before my father and I could put up the treehouse, we needed to carry its sections through brambles and over a stream in order to reach the site, deep in the woods. This step, along with putting the parts in the tree, we could not have done alone. One summer weekend, a few friends came up to New Hampshire with us. With their help, we schlepped the treehouse through the woods and up into the tree. We laughed and strained, taking breaks to joke around and play Frisbee. It was challenging work, but here we are now, standing in it for the first time.

I envision my friends sitting in the treehouse with me decades from now. Gray floorboards that once were red; the walls streaked with the orange of rusty old screws. Our children, maybe even grandchildren, are laughing and screaming with joy. Our communal experiences in this treehouse, the work and play shared with loved ones, have made the treehouse special to us.

Occasionally people ask me when I expect to finish building the treehouse. I tell them that I don't really know; it isn't the date of completion that matters. It's the process: the planning, the spending time with my father and friends, the hands-on building, and just being in the woods. This is what brings me joy.

ESSAY 2 (YALE SUPPLEMENT): WHAT IN PARTICULAR ABOUT YALE HAS INFLUENCED YOUR DECISION TO APPLY?

Yale appeals to me because I know without a doubt that I would receive a superb education there. In addition to its overall strength, Yale has renowned departments in the two fields in which I am most interested: math and art. Also, I feel that Yale is set apart from other high-caliber universities by its residential colleges. I have always been part of close communities that give me an important sense of belonging. I therefore believe that the intimate environment the residential colleges foster would be the perfect place for me to learn and grow.

ESSAY 3 (YALE SUPPLEMENT): SHORT TAKES

You have been granted a free weekend next month. How will you spend it?

I would spend it with my friends and family. After a long day of sledding we would sit inside in front of a fire, sipping tea and playing board games.

What is something about which you have changed your mind in the last three years?

I believed that strict gun control would alleviate gun violence in the US. I now see that in the foreseeable future this could not be a panacea.

What is the best piece of advice you have received while in high school?

Don't procrastinate. I have found that bad time management is the greatest factor preventing people from reaching their potential.

What do you wish you were better at being or doing?

Fluency in a second language would open up so much of the world to me. Lacking innate talent, I study that much harder to learn each new phrase.

What is a learning experience, in or out of the classroom, that has had a significant impact on you?

Joining the gymnastics team with no prior experience showed me that with great effort I can do incredible things that had been far beyond my ability.

ESSAY 4 (YALE SUPPLEMENT): IN THIS ESSAY, PLEASE REFLECT ON SOMETHING YOU WOULD LIKE US TO KNOW ABOUT YOU THAT WE MIGHT NOT LEARN FROM THE REST OF YOUR APPLICATION, OR ON SOMETHING ABOUT WHICH YOU WOULD LIKE TO SAY MORE. YOU MAY WRITE ABOUT ANYTHING—FROM PERSONAL EXPERIENCES OR INTERESTS TO INTELLECTUAL PURSUITS.

Iterate . . .
            Iterate . . .
                        Iterate . . .
                                    Iterate . . .

I could see the iterations of the function hop around the complex plane of the room. Some paths quickly whizzing off to infinity, others spiraling inwards, first to one sleeping body on the floor, inward to the next, and lastly inward to me to bounce around but never leave, me, the center of the fractal, dreaming, sprawled out on a fold-out couch.

Two summers ago, I attended Hampshire College Summer Studies in Mathematics (HCSSIM), a six-week residential program, to investigate higher-level math concepts. On our last night there, we knew that we probably would never see most of our newfound friends again, so we had no choice but to stay up all night and hang out for the last time. Not surprisingly, we eventually dozed off and turned into my fractalline dream.

Math has fascinated me ever since I started studying it in kindergarten. After my sophomore year, I had the opportunity to go to HCSSIM to study a wide variety of topics, ranging from number theory, group theory, graph theory, and even the study of formal theories themselves along with countless (though technically a finite and countable number of) other subjects. Never before had I studied mathematics so intensively and with such purpose. I could feel my thought processes change as I adapted from the civilian life to one of a mathematician.

My main focus at HCSSIM was the study of fractals and the functions that make them. This was all very interesting, but I did not feel that I really understood why the functions would create such shapes. Toward the end of the program, I had a revelation and fractals finally made sense to me. I spent the rest of my stay pondering the nature of this process and developing my thoughts on the formation of fractals. In thinking single-mindedly about fractals for days, they infiltrated my subconscious, and on my last night there, they manifested themselves in a dream.

Even before this revelation and this dream, math had been an important part of me, but only by the end of my time at HCSSIM did I realize how large a part. Although it is hard to say what the future holds, I intend to continue studying mathematics, so that I can reach those moments of sublime comprehension. I intend to go beyond simple proficiency and to truly appreciate the underlying concepts in all their depth. Only then will I be satisfied with my understanding.

Marianne Konikoff

Hometown: Baton Rouge, LA

Year: Senior

College: Trumbull

Major(s): Mathematics

Extracurriculars: Yale Undergraduate Math Society; Smart Women's Securities, Chief Investment Officer

PROFILE

Marianne Konikoff came to Yale from an all-girls Catholic high school of roughly eleven hundred students in her hometown of Baton Rouge, Louisiana. She spent her high school years participating in an array of extracurriculars, such as math team, debate, and science fairs—not to mention the astrophysics research she conducted at Louisiana State University throughout her last three years of high school.

Growing up, Marianne knew she wanted to leave Louisiana for college, and she fell in love with Yale when she toured the university the summer before her junior year of high school. Yale's residential college system, she says, reminded her of the close-knit high school she attended, where she enjoyed spirit weeks and competitions between graduating class years. She also knew she would be challenged and supported academically in New Haven: Although Yale is a liberal arts college, Marianne saw that Yale also boasts the resources of a large research institution for students interested in STEM.

During the summer before her senior year, Marianne traveled back to New Haven to take part in EXPLO at Yale—a pre-college program that allows students to take courses and attend workshops on campus. Setting her sights on becoming a Bulldog, Marianne applied early action to the university and committed soon after being accepted in December 2013.

Marianne looks back on her Yale years fondly. She certainly kept herself busy; she was the treasurer of the Yale Undergraduate Math Society, while running operations and registration for a high school math tournament held on Yale's campus. She also worked as a peer tutor for introductory math courses. Outside of Yale, she served as the chief investment officer for Smart Women's Securities, a nonprofit organization that teaches undergraduate women about personal and corporate finance.

During her college summers, Marianne spent her time studying at the London School of Economics and interning at Raymond James, an investment bank. After her junior year at Yale, Marianne interned at the consulting firm Altman Vilandrie in Boston, where she began working full-time in fall 2018.

Marianne's essays include her Common App personal statement.

ESSAY 1 (COMMON APP):
PERSONAL STATEMENT
Recount an incident or time when you experienced failure. How did it affect you, and what lessons did you learn?

I had my entire essay planned out. I was going to talk about the science fair, all of the unbelievably talented people I've met over the last four years, and how much I've grown from research and competition alike. I carefully listed every story, every point, every skill I wanted to include, remembering each fair and the friends, judges, conversations, and pizza parties that left their mark on me forever. Why shouldn't I be able to write about the most important part of my life and show essentially who I am along the way? I methodically organized and meticulously crafted it just as I would any research paper or critical analysis, but when I picked it up the next day, I realized that a vital element was missing: me.

I couldn't figure out what had gone wrong; I had done everything according to plan. The ineffectiveness of my trusted formula was discouraging, for I wasn't used to methodology failing me. Then I remembered what happened countless times before and will surely happen again: a crashing program, an erroneous code, a failure. Astrophysics and computer programming consumed the summer before my sophomore year as I began immersing myself in the world of science fairs and allowed myself to fully and completely fall in love with science. I will be eternally grateful to the professor who took a chance on an overly-enthusiastic fifteen year old girl who just wanted to learn something new. Although knowledge, friendship, networking, and passion for fields I never would have considered previously filled that summer and the years following, difficulties and disappointments made frequent appearances. Since it was my first time working in a truly collaborative research environment, my first experience with programming, and my first real job, I quickly learned the importance of perseverance and repeated trials. If a code didn't work, I searched for an error. If I couldn't find an error, I would try a difference approach. If neither option worked, then I finally began to accept that it was okay to ask for help, and often the simple act of talking about the issue with another person could help me solve the problem myself. As I spent more time in the science fair world, it became easier to acknowledge failure, look for a solution, and try again.

I stepped back from my essay and reassessed the situation. My original plan had a rather conspicuous flaw. A report of my time at fairs and symposia would not say anything about me; I needed a way to convey what they taught me and how they made me the inquisitive, open-minded conversationalist and scientist I have become. While discussing the present challenge with my mom, one common theme emerged from every thought: failure. After talking about it, I decided to take a different approach; instead of restricting what I've learned from science fair, I found a way to apply it to outside experiences. When I paused and honestly examined the little details of my life, I realized just how much science fair affects my decisions and the way in which I make them. It has permanently changed the way I interact with others, my ability to convey ideas clearly and effectively, and the ease with which I discuss everything from physics to pop culture with judges and peers alike, but most importantly, it taught me that failure is okay. It's normal, and if I try again, think innovatively, and ask for assistance when necessary, it will work out, even if the results aren't perfectly aligned with the original goal. Writing a six thousand word research paper flows naturally, so my initial inability to compose a six hundred word personal statement bothered me. Although I neglected to notice it at the time, one critical difference on which I so often rely separated the two: not everything can be calculated.

Angus Mossman

Hometown: Leland, WI

Year: Senior

College: Jonathan Edwards

Major(s): Ecology & Evolutionary Biology

Extracurriculars: Yale Outdoors

PROFILE

Angus Mossman says his hometown of Leland, Wisconsin, had thirty-five people, two bars, and a church.

"There are way more deer and bald eagles in the area than there are people," he says.

Angus grew up in south-central Wisconsin and attended Sauk Prairie High School, an eight-hundred-person school about fifteen miles down the road from his home. He dabbled in athletics, playing tennis and running cross country, and played bassoon in the band. His passion for music—coupled with a love of nature that his parents, wildlife biologists by profession, had ingrained in him from an early age—has stayed with him throughout his life.

Angus had always assumed he would go to the University of Wisconsin–Madison, the highest achieving state school and the institution of choice for college-matriculating students at his school. But during his senior year, his mom brought home an anthology of the top colleges across the country. Although Angus began flipping through its monstrous pages only to appease her, he says he never would have ended up at Yale without that enormous book.

The book broadened Angus's horizons, but friendly competition with a friend in his AP Physics class pushed him further down the path to seriously looking into Yale. In his senior year science class, his friend joked about having received her Yale recruitment letter in the mail. Short of knowing the school existed, he only remembered that the last time a person from his school attended the institution had been sometime in the 1960s. He knew nothing more about Yale, not to mention what "Ivy League" meant.

But his classmate had inspired him. Angus went home, looked up Yale in that big book of colleges, and saw notes of hefty financial aid, a solid study abroad program, and large numbers of international students. As a student interested in travel and international studies, Yale's offerings, along with its smaller size, appealed to him. He applied to Yale and the University of Wisconsin–Madison and was admitted into both.

Bulldog Days, Yale's admitted students' event, sealed his decision. Angus says that his visit made him understand why people thought of Yale as their home. Specifically, he recalls playing music in the Branford common room with some of the students who would later form a band with him at Yale.

At Yale, Angus truly found his niche in Yale Outdoors, the folk music community, and various foraging activities (through the Yale Farm and otherwise). Academically, he enjoyed the university's liberal arts focus, which allowed him to study topics unrelated to his major in Ecology & Evolutionary Biology. Despite Angus's strong interest in the major, its classes were not among his favorites at Yale, as their confinement to the classroom made him feel cut off from the nature they studied. During his junior and senior years, he enrolled in classes at the School of Forestry and Environmental Studies, allowing him to explore New Haven's nature as he had desired. He befriended people through these classes and extracurriculars and opted to move off campus, away from his residential college of Jonathan Edwards, to live with friends from Yale Outdoors.

After graduating last fall, Angus moved back to Wisconsin to work with various local landowners in the area. He looks to begin work as a teaching fellow next year.

Angus's essays include his Common App personal statement.

ESSAY 1 (COMMON APP):
PERSONAL STATEMENT

Biting into a sun-warmed tomato fresh off the vine is one of the best things I've ever done. It is just as good to sit around the wood stove eating steaming homemade applesauce made from fruit off of my trees while an ongoing blizzard shakes the windowpanes and blankets the yard in fresh snow. I've lived with a vegetable garden on my family's rural home all my life and have spent countless hours cultivating, harvesting, and preserving the wide variety of organic vegetables and fruits we grow: from cantaloupes to carrots and beans to bok choy. I'm always amazed at the difference between a cucumber from the garden and a store-bought one. A home-grown, well, anything has so much more flavor than the same item from a store. Knowing where my food comes from is reassuring, and when I go to the pantry to pull out some preserved food I think about where it came from and all the experiences that went with it. Gardening and using what the land provides made me interested in a sustainable lifestyle. I try to live as earth-friendly as possible and steer others in this direction, whether by recycling, carpooling, or buying locally. I believe everyone deserves the opportunity of eating local produce fresh off the land, and sharing food from my garden is one way for me to give others this opportunity. It's so satisfying to give my retired neighbors a basket of rhubarb and green beans and to watch their eyes light up and their lips form a grin. Besides visiting with the neighbors, gardening has given me a chance to spend time with and learn from my parents. They have taught me so much about gardening and many life lessons during the hours we spend in the garden and kitchen preparing and preserving the bounty from the land. Working the land and eating the produce from it has been important to me since I was a child and even more so as I grew older and more interested in sustainable living. Eating a whole meal from the local land is inspiring, knowing that all the work I've put into the produce has paid off in the wonderful array of colors that covers the plate before me. But today the garden isn't just a place to grow my own food; it presents a great educational opportunity for everyone. Because a garden has so much to offer, in the future I hope I can continue to share my experiences with others, especially that of a freshly picked, sun-warmed tomato.

Katherine Oh

Hometown: New York City, NY

Year: Senior

College: Silliman

Major(s): Psychology

Extracurriculars: Danceworks;
Korean American Students at Yale;
UNITY Korean Drum Troupe

PROFILE

Katherine Oh knew when she began the college application process that she wanted to find a place where students were supportive of each other. She found that place at Yale, where she graduated in 2018 as a psychology major.

"[Yale] did give me what I was looking for. It was a nurturing environment," she says.

Katherine attended Stuyvesant High School in New York City, where, outside of the classroom, she focused on math and Korean traditional dance. Eager to promote diversity in her school's math team, Katherine was not only a teammate but also a trusted mentor, motivator, and friend to the younger girls on the team. After making the move to college, however, Katherine spent most of her time exploring new interests and extracurriculars. She became a psychology major and experimented with new forms of dance with Danceworks, a multigenre student dance ensemble.

Even after graduating from Yale, Katherine is continuing to explore new passions. She studied in Beijing during the summer after her senior year and is currently spending an academic year studying Chinese in Taipei.

Katherine is taking this time to reflect. "I've come to realize what I don't want and that my interest was really in discovering what I liked in life," she says.

Katherine says that becoming involved in different groups on campus as an undergraduate helped her discover her passions. She also became involved in the Korean American and Asian American communities, which helped her embrace her Korean heritage and learn about issues like Asian American activism that she was unfamiliar with in high school.

"It's not always in the classroom that you learn new things. It's through your peers and your community that you learn new things," she notes.

In fact, Katherine says that one of her favorite parts of Yale was the student community itself. Forging through college alone is "really hard" and, having a supportive community "really made my Yale experience," she explains.

Katherine also emphasizes that despite the stress most college students experience, "in the end, everything works out." She adds that canceling out stress and maintaining a healthy mindset is imperative.

"That's what I would want to tell any future Yalies and current students—just that some of the hardest times at Yale you're going to feel like you're going to fail . . . but at the end of the day, you realize you're just as fine as everyone else, and you've made it to this really incredible university," she says.

Katherine's essays include her Common App personal statement and one of her Yale supplemental essays.

ESSAY 1 (COMMON APP):
PERSONAL STATEMENT

In October of 2000, at the eighteenth annual New York Korean Festival, I trailed behind my mother as I voraciously scarfed

down my corn dog. My wandering eyes landed upon a gran-
diose stage, where two young women in opulent, full-length,
red silk dresses were twirling their paper fans. Mouth agape, I
squeezed my mom's hand as tightly as a four-year-old possibly
could, and begged to take dance lessons.

Apparently, I hadn't been the only one awed by the gorgeous
costumes that day. The following weekend, in a studio in Flushing, Queens, I entered a room packed with other eager, young
aspirants.

After each lesson, I was amazed at how much precision was
required to be considered even mediocre when performing this
art. From perfecting the width of our footsteps to hitting the
same angle between our forearm and bicep, I practiced for fifteen hours a week to make these complicated moves appear
simple and natural. I even had an entire class devoted solely to
our breathing techniques: how to inhale with our entire bodies,
how to hold that breath with our core muscles, how to match
the timing of my breathing with everyone else's. Needless to say,
many of my elementary-school-aged classmates started dropping
like flies, but I remained intrigued by the challenge to make the
difficult look beautiful.

Moving on to middle school, our ranks continued to be dec-
imated as classmates were lured away to mainstream dance
genres, from ballet to hip hop. When I'd run into them in my
Asian-American enclave of Flushing, they would poke fun at me
for sticking with the old-school dance that our grandmothers had
performed. Still, I maintained that Korean dance was more than
just alternating the pace of my footsteps to express a specific
emotion in one split second. I was drawn to this activity since
it made me a cultural ambassador not just to non-Koreans, but
also to Korean-Americans who weren't aware of this particular
facet of our shared heritage.

But, when I enrolled at Stuyvesant, my mother's requests for
me to help out in her Chelsea convenience deli grew louder. She
asked me to quit dance since it was just a hobby that wouldn't

help me get into college. Although I understood her practical attitude, I knew dance was too important for me to give up. Since I see myself as a role model for other youth, particularly when I teach workshops at local schools, I implored her to think about which activity best portrays the image of immigrant Koreans: working behind the cash register selling gum, or performing on stage in front of non-Koreans and sharing one of our treasured customs. We struck a compromise: I'd continue to dance, but commit to one evening shift a week.

This past April, one of my close friends recruited me for Stuyvesant's Culture Festival. Performing in front of hundreds, I was nervous that the audience might not appreciate this relatively unknown art. However, their booming applause proved just the opposite. That weekend, my confidence still soaring, I volunteered to perform at my Queens studio for a visiting class of ten young African-American girls from a Bronx Charter school. I was overjoyed when the second graders eagerly approached me afterwards not only to touch my ruby embroidered dress, but also to learn more about the stories behind my dances. Thus, sharing my heritage with those from outside of my cultural demographic and seeing their sincere interest confirmed for me that the past thirteen years of twirling and focused breathing have been well worth the effort.

ESSAY 2 (YALE SUPPLEMENT): PLEASE REFLECT ON SOMETHING YOU WOULD LIKE US TO KNOW ABOUT YOU THAT WE MIGHT NOT LEARN FROM THE REST OF YOUR APPLICATION, OR ON SOMETHING ABOUT WHICH YOU WOULD LIKE TO SAY MORE.

I was within earshot when Aaron groaned to Brad and Chris, senior members of Stuyvesant's math team, that, "even though I'm better at math, colleges are going to take Katherine over me just because she's a girl." Earlier, I had considered asking their advice on how to compute $f(0)$ when the quadratic polynomial f(x) has a real zero at x=2, and when f(f(x)) has only one real zero at x=5, but hearing this chauvinism, I tackled the ARML question by myself.

The following Saturday, Ally hosted the fencing team's first sleepover of the season at her luxurious condominium. We sprawled out on her bed to watch our perennial favorite, *Mean Girls,* which was a particular treat since I rarely commandeered my home's sole television from my overworked father.

I started to anticipate the part of the movie when Cady recognizes that "the limit does not exist" and clinches the win for her team; I had joined the math team hoping to experience similar intellectual triumphs. Unfortunately, the hypercompetitive clique of Aaron, Brad, and Chris became my own version of the "Plastics." After they befriended me in my freshman year, their barbs quickly came out once our coach started placing me on the upper-level teams. Feeling that my presence undermined their entrenched pecking order, the three would arrogantly mock me as inferior, or worse, claim that as a girl, I enjoyed special treatment.

Interestingly, after watching *Mean Girls* at Ally's that night, I had an epiphany: I needed to stop seeking Cady's glorious victory and instead embrace my role as the ever-enthusiastic "pusher," Ms. Norbury. I focused on how much pride I take in providing a support system for teammates, especially younger female members whose skins haven't thickened the way mine has over the past three years. Knowing how difficult it was for me to drown out the negativity of certain team members in the early weeks, I approached our coach in my junior fall and asked if I could personally mentor incoming novices.

After he named me one of his NYC team captains, I hit the ground running at the first practice. Seeing Jasmine, a freshman, sitting alone as her three male teammates huddled to solve a problem, I waved her over and advised, "You belong in that group. Never forget that and don't let them forget it." She sheepishly smiled as my supportive nod encouraged her to join the group without their invitation. At that weekend's tournament, I saw Jasmine sitting alone again, despondent after she had scored a 3/10 on a mock test. Patting her on the back, I slyly pointed to Aaron and said, "That senior who just pulled off a 9/10 got a 2/10 when he was your age." Her smile reminded me why I push myself to surmount the obstacles that others put in my way because of my gender.

Rosa Vargas

Hometown: San Diego, CA

Year: Senior

College: Timothy Dwight

Major(s): Ethics, Politics & Economics

Extracurriculars: Timothy Dwight, head of college aide; Pi Beta Phi sorority

PROFILE

Rosa Vargas is an Ethics, Politics, & Economics major from San Diego, California, who recently graduated from Yale. Her college essays highlight a long-lived interest in immigration and policy, which she continued to pursue at Yale. After volunteering for Amigos de las Americas in high school, she brought her passion for service with her to college, and she became active in groups such as the Yale Democrats and Latina Women at Yale. Rosa also enrolled in Directed Studies in her first year of college.

Rosa was drawn to Yale because of the strong community, especially within the residential college system. She helped to create that community by becoming involved as a buttery worker and office aide at Timothy Dwight residential college. Rosa also joined the sorority Pi Beta Phi and played club volleyball. One of her favorite memories at Yale was the Yale–Harvard game. She remembers the joy she felt experiencing the school spirit of her classmates. She has attended all but one home football game during her time at Yale, and loved seeing everyone have the same enthusiasm for the sports teams as when they played against Harvard.

Rosa's experiences with academic advising at Yale also had a major influence on her senior year. She was unsure of her postgraduation plans until the summer after Commencement. The dean of Timothy Dwight and other academic advisers helped her decide to take at least one year off before law school. In the two years between undergrad and law school, Rosa worked as a pro bono program assistant at Casa Cornelia Law Center, an immigration law firm in San Diego.

Rosa's essays include her Common App personal statement and one of her Yale supplemental essays.

ESSAY 1 (COMMON APP):
PERSONAL STATEMENT
Some students have a background or story that is so central to them that they believe their application would be incomplete without it. If this sounds like you, please share your story.

One of my first memories is trying to figure out how to pray to Allah. My parents had just adopted a Muslim family from Kosovo who barely escaped ethnic cleansing. I learned we would not be praying our usual prayers so we could make the new family living with us feel welcome. Now I was praying to a new God and listening to two adults and two children of six and eight years old who only spoke Albanian and Serbo-Croatian.

This type of experience was commonplace in my life. I was born into a politically active family three weeks after my father tried and failed to become the first Latino ever elected to the US Congress to represent the California–Mexico border. It would take him three more attempts and three more elections to win. I grew up on protest marches against poverty, racism, inequality, and a lack of compassion for immigrants. I spent many weekends either placing jugs of water in the California desert for immigrants trying to cross the border undetected or on precinct walks first being carried, then walking by myself, and finally leading others.

My parents made a conscious decision to live in a high-crime neighborhood to make a difference for the people who live there, which meant that from an early age, I was exposed to the deep challenges our country and neighborhoods face. When my father led the San Diego City Council Public Safety Committee, he helped initiate community policing, placed more street lights on dangerous corners, and organized community trash pick-up days, making our neighborhood a much safer place to live. However, my father's commitment and principles have come at a cost to my family. I was never allowed to play outside our house unsupervised because of the danger of gangs and drugs. My father's push for change has resulted in threats against our family, even to the extent that the police needed to be stationed outside of our house for protection.

The commitment shown by my family informs the decisions I make every day. For a short period of time I played club volleyball, and it helped bring out the competitive spirit I knew I had in me, but I gave it up when I heard about a program, Amigos de las Americas, that needed volunteers to travel to Latin America during the summers to help the poor and marginalized. I raised money for the needed projects by selling chocolate and Nicaraguan coffee.

My first year with the Amigos program, I trained all year on topics such as leadership, cultural sensitivity and health and safety. That summer, I traveled to Los Lipes, a jungle community in Nicaragua, to improve water purification for the community. During these six weeks I was immersed in the culture and fell in love with the people there; the experience was so rewarding that although it is unusual to sign up for a second year, I did. As a veteran volunteer, the next year I trained and then traveled to Santa Elena, Paraguay, to work in an isolated, indigenous community. Finally, as a senior, I am now training others to do similar work in other Latin American countries.

I don't know what my life would have been if it was filled with Saturday soccer games instead of delivering water jugs in the California desert. When I was younger I would often think of how different my life was from the lives of my friends at school. I was embarrassed that my family lived in the barrio; none of my friends knew the homeless by name like I did. Now I wear my experiences like a crown. I love the upbringing I had and I cannot wait to get a college education to continue solving the problems of the real world.

ESSAY 2 (YALE SUPPLEMENT): IN THIS ESSAY, PLEASE REFLECT ON SOMETHING YOU WOULD LIKE US TO KNOW ABOUT YOU THAT WE MIGHT NOT LEARN FROM THE REST OF YOUR APPLICATION, OR ON SOMETHING ABOUT WHICH YOU WOULD LIKE TO SAY MORE. YOU MAY WRITE ABOUT ANYTHING—FROM PERSONAL EXPERIENCES OR INTERESTS TO INTELLECTUAL PURSUITS.

My first day in Paraguay went like this: I took a bus for forty minutes from the town of Villarica to the edge of a community called San Luis off a long dirt road. I walked for thirty minutes until I met up in the center of San Luis with a seventy-nine-year-old lady and her granddaughter, neither of whom spoke Spanish nor wore shoes—despite the fact that we had an hour hike in front of us to the mountain community of Santa Elena. I walked that last hour with my companions in the hot sun carrying my belongings past stray dogs, cats, pigs, horses, cows, and chickens.

I was a volunteer for Amigos de las Americas, a mini Peace Corps that sends students to impoverished areas of Latin America. Volunteering in a rural community in Latin America may not have been a common aspiration for most fifteen year olds, but it was my dream; I overcame my fears and garnered the courage within me to do it. My first summer I volunteered for six weeks in Los Lipes, Nicaragua, and although it is uncommon to volunteer for a second year, I did, this time in Paraguay.

My summers in both communities in which I worked consisted of teaching health, environment, and self-esteem related subjects at the school each day and working with the local community to solve water purification problems.

The people in Nicaragua and Paraguay taught me much more than I ever taught them. Although they often lacked running water, electricity, latrines, or reliable roads, they had all they needed in strong families and compassion for people even poorer than themselves. In Paraguay, the people in my village even had their own language—Guarani. This experience has brought out the courage and confidence within me to more seriously solve the problems of the real world starting with my own community.